More Praise for *Living Like You Mean It*

"Where shall we run if we run from ourselves? This book asks us to look anew at our models of health and happiness and to realize that personal liberation is not possible if we are not at liberty to feel what we feel. Through stories and examples, Ron Frederick walks us through that issue in a way that is simple, clear, and focused and that has a chance to fundamentally change human lives."

—Steven C. Hayes, foundation professor, Department of Psychology, University of Nevada, and author, *Get Out of Your Mind and Into Your Life*

"Written like he means it—and clearly he does—Ron Frederick's book is a gift, written by a master clinician and an amazing person. His heart and soul, his humor and sparkling intelligence, his pathos and practicality, are all there from the great title to the very last word. Down to earth and with a twinkle in his eyes, Ron Frederick is the guide and companion you have been looking for. As he passionately makes clear: you can shed your resignation and vitality and joy can be yours again. And as you journey to reconnect with yourself and those you love—you will not be alone. Step by step, you feel him with you, steady and wise. What a great book! I will recommend it to my patients and friends alike. And, what's more, I can't wait to read it again."

—Diana Fosha, Ph.D., director, the AEDP Institute, and author, *The Transforming Power of Affect*

"Dr. Frederick's wise and powerful book is an inspiration. It is also a practical guide to help us feel more deeply, face our fears more confidently, and live each moment more fully."

—Dr. Larina Kase, author, *The Confident Leader* and the *New York Times* best seller *The Confident Speaker*

"Dr. Frederick's first book demonstrates his gift of communicating in an accessible, human, meaningful manner about one of life's most important mysteries—the true value and purpose of our emotions. He shows us how to navigate the guidance system they provide on the road to happiness, fulfillment, and depth in our lives. Hopefully, this will be the first of many books from this gifted writer."

—Joseph Bailey, licensed psychologist and
best-selling author of *Fearproof Your Life*
and *Slowing Down to the Speed of Life*

"It is a delight to read a book on emotions that integrates so much of the cutting-edge research in brain, body, mind, and attachment. Ron Fredrick has managed to take difficult concepts and translate them into language that is understandable. This is a book for those who seek to reconnect with their own emotions, and with the emotions of people they care about. I highly recommend *Living Like You Mean It*."

—Marion Solomon, Ph.D., director,
Clinical Training, Lifespan Learning Institute,
and author, *Lean on Me*

Living LIKE YOU MEAN IT

Use the Wisdom and Power of Your Emotions
to Get the Life You Really Want

Ronald J. Frederick, PhD

 JOSSEY-BASS
A Wiley Imprint
www.josseybass.com

Published by Jossey-Bass
A Wiley Imprint
989 Market Street, San Francisco, CA 94103-1741—www.josseybass.com

Readers should be aware that Internet Web sites offered as citations and/or sources for further
information may have changed or disappeared between the time this was written and when it is read.

The lines "I am a rock, I am an island" and "And a rock feels no pain; and an island never cries" are
from "I Am a Rock," recorded and released by Simon & Garfunkel in 1965. Copyright © 1965 by
Paul Simon.

Excerpt from "The Road Not Taken" is from *The Poetry of Robert Frost,* edited by Edward Connery
Lathem. Copyright © 1916, 1969 by Henry Holt & Company. Copyright © 1944 by Robert Frost.
Reprinted by permission of Henry Holt & Company, LLC.

Jossey-Bass books and products are available through most bookstores. To contact Jossey-Bass directly
call our Customer Care Department within the U.S. at 800-956-7739, outside the U.S. at 317-572-3986,
or fax 317-572-4002.

Jossey-Bass also publishes its books in a variety of electronic formats. Some content that appears in
print may not be available in electronic books.

Library of Congress Cataloging-in-Publication Data
Frederick, Ronald J. (date).
    Living like you mean it : use the wisdom and power of your emotions to get the life you really
want / Ronald J. Frederick. — 1st ed.
      p.   cm.
    Includes bibliographical references and index.
    ISBN 978-0-470-37703-1 (cloth)
      1. Emotions.   2. Success—Psychological aspects.   I. Title.
BF511.F74   2009
152.4—dc22

2008041907

Printed in the United States of America
FIRST EDITION
HB Printing 10 9 8 7 6 5 4 3 2 1

CONTENTS

To my family,
By birth and by choice

ACKNOWLEDGMENTS

WHEN I STARTED DOWN THE PATH OF WRITING this book five years ago, I had no idea what the journey would entail. I couldn't have gone the distance alone. It is with deep gratitude that I thank the following people who, in their own special way, have helped me make this book a reality:

Dan Ambrosio, my literary agent at Vigliano Associates, for his belief in this project from the beginning; for his energy, enthusiasm, and support; and for shepherding me through this process with aplomb. I couldn't have asked for a better advocate.

Sheryl Fullerton, my editor at Jossey-Bass, for her deep appreciation and understanding of my message (and helping me convey it in far fewer words); her excellent suggestions; her steady, guiding hand; and her professional integrity. It's been a joy to work with her.

The wonderful team at Jossey-Bass, for their humanity, hard work, and commitment to excellence.

Katherine Crowley, of K Squared Enterprises, for knowing I had this book in me before I did, for being there for me at just the right moments, and for introducing me to Dan Ambrosio.

Mark Chimsky, Mark Levy, and Mary Carroll Moore, who, early on, lent their literary expertise to the proposal, and helped give it wings.

Larina Kase, of Performance & Success Coaching, for her wonderful guidance, enthusiasm, and generosity.

The many family members, friends, and colleagues who generously read the manuscript at various stages in its development, discussed its content, and provided me with invaluable feedback and encouragement. In particular, Tim Beyer, Kim Frederick, Jackie Frederick-Berner (who also came up with the title, *Living Like You Mean It*), Diana Fosha, SueAnne Piliero, Sara Beyer (who also created the diagrams in Chapter Four), Donna Fraser, Noah Glassman, Ben Lipton, Natasha Prenn, Danny Yeung, Belinda Boscardin, Stacey Kirchner, Jenny Moore, and Christopher Szarke.

The many teachers and talented therapists who have inspired me, shaped my thinking, and fostered my clinical development. Especially, Diana Fosha, Leigh McCullough, Isabel Sklar, Jill Strunk, Gil Tunnell, Michael Laikin, Terry Sheldon, Maria Derevenco, John Budin, members of the International Experiential Dynamic Therapy Association, and my colleagues at the Accelerated Experiential Dynamic Psychotherapy Institute.

My students, for challenging me to put my thinking and approach into words, inspiring me with their talent and desire to learn, and helping me grow both as a teacher and clinician.

My clients, for allowing me into their hearts and lives, honoring me with their deepest feelings, and inspiring me with their courage. It's a privilege to be a part of their journeys.

The staff at Park House, for their caring hearts and delightful sense of humor.

Susan Schaefer, trusted guide, for being there when the road got tough and helping me be able to be present for the good stuff.

Diana Fosha, therapist extraordinaire, for teaching me, from the "bottom-up," about the transforming power of emotion and, in the doing, helped change the course of my life. This book wouldn't exist had it not been for the work we did together. Her continued support, generosity, and friendship are a gift.

My friends, for their frequent check-ins, words of encouragement, and rescuing me from my laptop.

My family, for their love and support, for their steadfast belief in me, and for making me laugh like no one else.

Finally, Tim Beyer, a better partner I couldn't have imagined if I tried. I thank him, quite simply, for everything.

To protect confidentiality, the people described in this book are composites of many different clients with whom I have worked. Names and essential identifying characteristics are fictitious, and any resemblance to a single person is coincidental.

The best and most beautiful things in the world
cannot be seen or even touched.
They must be felt with the heart.

—HELEN KELLER

INTRODUCTION

CONSIDERING THAT YOU'VE PICKED UP THIS BOOK and are reading it right now, it's probably safe to say that, in some way, you're feeling dissatisfied with your life. However, when you look at the facts, they don't quite add up to a life that's lacking. Your days are busy and full. You have friends, work colleagues, family, maybe even a partner or spouse. Yet something just doesn't seem right. Something's missing.

Many of us feel this way. We long to be more alive and present in our lives, more in touch with ourselves, and closer to those we love. Yet no matter what we do, we can't seem to get there. We wonder why we're unhappy. Why our relationships aren't more satisfying. Why life isn't more gratifying. We wonder, *Is this as good as it gets?*

Some argue that our busy lives are to blame. We have stressful jobs, work long hours, and endure grueling commutes. We face increased time pressures, household responsibilities, and family demands. We're too pressed to slow down and live more mindfully. We don't have the time it takes to get together with friends and family and really invest in our relationships. Our energy is too sapped to allow us to step into our lives in a more meaningful way.

These things may all appear true, but I'm convinced there's more going on than just being busy.

From my experiences with the many people I've seen in my psychotherapy and coaching practice, with the people I encounter in my life both professionally and personally, and in my own life, I've come to believe that a big piece of what is making us feel disconnected has to do with fear.

What are we afraid of? The answer may surprise you. We're afraid of our own feelings.

Our feelings are what make us feel alive and vital, energize us to meet and deal with life's challenges, and point us in the best direction to get what we really want. Our feelings are what bridge the gap between ourselves and others, enliven our relationships, and help us feel close. And it's a *feelings phobia*—our fear of and discomfort with our feelings and our inability to share them with others—that keeps us detached from the wisdom and power inside us, and at a distance from others.

This kind of fear is actually quite common. In fact, most of us are afraid of our feelings. We're afraid to feel the full extent of our emotions and afraid of being emotionally alive and present with others. We're afraid of being vulnerable, of drawing attention to ourselves, of looking like a fool. We're afraid of being overwhelmed, of losing control, of getting out of hand. We're afraid of being seen for who we really are.

So what do we do? We avoid our feelings and do everything we can to steer clear of them, to keep them hidden. We distract

---

For Better or Worse

When we suppress our feelings, they don't just go away. They fester inside, drain us of vital energy, and eventually resurface as

Anxiety	Worry
Fear	Restlessness
Hyperactivity	Depression
Irritability	Lack of motivation
Procrastination	Chronic fatigue
Insomnia	Hypertension
Stomach and intestinal problems	Headaches
Teeth grinding	Angry outbursts
Relationship problems	Sexual difficulties
Poor self-esteem	Emptiness

---

ourselves, push our feelings aside, stuff them back in, and hope they'll go away.

But they don't. They keep trying to get our attention, to be heard, to be responded to—that's their nature. They reemerge as the sense that something is off, odd, or not right; as worry, irritability, restlessness, anxiety, or depression.

Do we listen to them then? No. We work harder at avoiding them. We throw ourselves into our work, or we shop, drink, eat, use drugs, have sex, or exercise fanatically. We talk on our cell phones, send messages on our BlackBerries, surf the Net, play video games, zone out in front of the television. Anything to keep us occupied, distracted. Anything to numb the fear we feel when we get close to our true feelings.

Instead of living like we really mean it, we move ahead on autopilot, only half alive, vaguely aware of what's going on inside us. We're clueless about how much we're getting in our own way, and we wonder why we're unhappy. Why isn't life more gratifying? Why aren't our relationships satisfying? Why do we feel so alone?

Nothing in this picture is going to change until we find the courage to face and share our feelings.

WHY THIS BOOK?

How do I understand this predicament so well? Been there, done that!

For so long, I was fairly out of touch with what I truly felt deep down inside, on a gut level. I had become so afraid of my emotions, of listening to and trusting my true feelings, that I couldn't hear the voice of my deepest self buried somewhere inside me— the voice that knew what I wanted, knew what I longed for, knew what felt right to me and what felt wrong.

I can say this to you now with the wisdom of hindsight, but at the time, I had no idea what was going on. I had no awareness of how anxious I was under the surface, no sense of how significantly fear was affecting every part of my life. My constant running—from home, to work, to school, to the gym, and home again—was fueled by a deep-seated, underlying fear of my emotions. It was this fear that kept me from my real feelings and prevented me from connecting more deeply with others.

What I *was* aware of was how alone I felt. Despite my busy life, a partner, friends, family, people I thought I was close to, something was amiss. I'd spend time with people, and afterward I'd walk away feeling empty, longing for connection, but not knowing what got in the way. *Was it something I was doing? Was it something I said? Do they just not like me or find me interesting?* I couldn't put my finger on it or figure out why I ended up feeling so alone.

So I kept up a pace, going round and round like a hamster on a wheel, doubting my sense that the relationship I was in just wasn't right, and running from the feelings I barely knew were there—my deep-seated fears about trusting my heart and moving forward in my life in a more authentic way. I did anything I could to keep from stopping and listening to my inner self, from really being present, because if I were to be still, I would have to face my fears and take the risk of honoring my feelings and claiming my life, and that just felt too scary.

I might have gone on like this forever had I not gotten the help I needed to recognize what, in fact, I really was afraid of—my true feelings—and to learn how to overcome my fears, embrace my emotional self, and really connect with others. I shudder to think where I might be now had I not heeded this wake-up call and begun to open up to my emotions.

In my work, I see so many people who are like I used to be, perhaps like yourself. Most of them have tried to change, have tried for years to do things differently. Some of them have even been in therapy before. But no matter how hard they tried, they weren't able to achieve any lasting success. Invariably, they ended up repeating the same patterns over and over again. Patterns that kept them cut off from their emotional selves and at a distance from others. Patterns that got them nowhere.

Sound familiar?

The reason for this repetitiveness is clear: no real change in how we feel or how we behave is going to take place until we deal with our feelings. If we really want things to change, if we really want to feel alive and connected to the people in our lives, we're going to have to learn to connect with and manage our feelings—the sadness we feel at our losses, the anger we feel when we're wronged, the joy we feel when we triumph, the love we feel when we care deeply, and everything in between.

Now, I know there are plenty of well-meaning people out there who will tell you otherwise. There are numerous books on the market about how to "rise above" your feelings, block them with your thoughts, or transform them through saying affirmations. Unfortunately, these strategies are insufficient and bring only short-term relief. And now we know why.

For years, cognitive science, or the science of the mind, dominated our understanding of the human psyche. Everywhere we turned, the overarching message we received from self-help books, talk shows, advice columns, and even some therapists was something along the lines of *just think positive.*

Let's be realistic. If it were that simple, we'd all be better by now, and I'd be running a bed-and-breakfast somewhere on Cape Cod!

Fortunately, in the last few years, there has been a virtual explosion of studies on emotion that are revolutionizing our understanding of how the brain works, develops, and changes. We now know that emotions can play a more powerful role than thoughts in bringing about well-being and lasting change. The reason for this is simple. Our feelings can arise much faster and be more intense than our thoughts. At times, no matter what we do to suppress them or how hard we try to control them, they'll have the edge. (I'll say more about why this is so in the next chapter.) In addition, recent discoveries in the field of neuroplasticity— the study of how the brain is able to change its structures and functions—reveal that emotional experience actually has the power to rewire our brain!

Doesn't it make sense for us to learn how to work with our feelings rather than work against them?

We also now know that as Daniel Goleman says in his best-selling book *Social Intelligence,* in a very basic way we are "wired to connect."[1] From the time we're born, it is our innate tendency to connect emotionally with others. And for good reason. The sense of security and safety that comes from emotional closeness is fundamental to our well-being. It provides us with what renowned psychiatrist John Bowlby described as a "secure base,"[2] a solid foundation from which we can grow and can explore the world. Relationships not only make us feel good but also enhance our ability to deal with stress and weather life's travails. They provide innumerable health benefits as well, enhancing immune, cardio-vascular, and brain functioning. In fact, people with close, supportive relationships actually live longer!

But there is a qualifier here. What matters most is not how many relationships you have but the quality of your relationships—that is, how emotionally close they are. In short, the closer we are, the more we benefit. And true closeness is possible only when we feel emotionally healthy, open, secure, and aware of our feelings and how they affect us. It thus behooves us to nurture our capacity to feel and connect in a healthy way by becoming more comfortable with our feelings and learning how to share them. If we don't, we're destined to feel disconnected and alone.

As you consider that perhaps you're not as comfortable with your feelings as you thought, the prospect of opening up more deeply to yourself and others may seem scary. I can certainly appreciate your concern. It *can* be scary. Many things are scary before you try them, but they can become things you later benefit from and enjoy doing, once you see that they aren't really that threatening. The same thing can happen with your feelings. The more you give them a try, the more you work at connecting to them, the easier the process gets, and the more adept you become at handling them.

So are you going to let fear keep you in the back row of your life, watching it play out before you on a distant movie screen, never really feeling a part of it, never really feeling close to your loved ones? Or would you rather feel more present and engaged in your life? Would you like your life to be more fulfilling?

If you're willing, I'm here to help. You'll have to be willing to give it a real shot and take some risks, to roll up your sleeves and get a little dirty, because it does take some work.

And although I can't promise you that it won't be painful or get messy at times, I can tell you this: learning to be with and share your feelings will transform your life in ways you never imagined possible. I know this personally, and I see it every day with my clients.

Here's what I've seen when people open up to their feelings:

- Their overall anxiety level is reduced, which brings great relief.

- They no longer feel stuck. Rather, they notice a sense of flow, of movement, of positive energy running through them. It's an energy that enlivens them, makes them feel stronger and more empowered. An energy that moves them to open up, to break through old barriers, and to experience themselves anew.
- They're in touch with and able to express their personal truth, a truth they no longer doubt. And by speaking up and giving voice to their feelings, they deepen and improve their relationships. They no longer feel alone.
- Their lives become richer and more gratifying, and they feel a profound sense of meaning, purpose, and belonging.

Ultimately, they come to realize their true potential to feel fully alive, vital, and deeply connected to their experience of themselves, others, and the world.

What greater reward could there be?

It is so gratifying to be part of such an amazing experience, to help someone discover and embrace the wonderful fully feeling person he or she was born to be. Not a day goes by that I'm not deeply moved as yet another person begins to break through the barriers that have kept him or her constricted and to connect with a deeper, fuller self-experience.

The more people I've been able to help, and the more I witness the dramatic changes that can take place when we develop the ability to be with and share our feelings, the more I have felt compelled to spread the word to others. I guess you might say that it's become a mission: to help people overcome their fears, awaken to the emotional richness inside them, and feel more intimately connected to the people in their lives. I am writing this book in the hopes of reaching you as well.

ABOUT THIS BOOK

Living Like You Mean It is designed to help you overcome your fears and be able to use the wisdom and power of your emotions to get the life you really want. I'm going to share with you what I learned and developed over the years, and what I teach my clients every day: a proven four-step approach to overcoming fear and connecting more deeply with yourself and others.

This book is divided into two sections. The first section, "Preparation," lays the foundation for the action steps that follow. We begin by getting very specific about the matter at hand: a fear of our feelings, or what I call *feelings phobia*. I'll outline the most common signs of this fear so that you can begin to recognize it in yourself. Next we'll take a look at how we come to be afraid of our feelings and of connecting more deeply with others. We'll also explore the emotional environment in which you grew up and the unwritten rules that may be governing your life now.

What then follows in the second section, "Taking Action," is my four-step approach to overcoming feelings phobia.

Step One: Becoming Aware

Making a change starts with cultivating what I call *emotional mindfulness*—your present-moment awareness of your feelings (which is covered in Chapter Three) as well as the things you do to avoid them (covered in Chapter Four). You need to turn your attention inward and begin to tune in to your emotional experience. You also need to recognize what it is you're doing that's getting in your way of being more in touch with yourself and others. We all have common patterns of behavior or "defenses" that we both knowingly and unknowingly use to avoid our feelings. For instance, when sadness starts to rise up inside, we may do things to try to keep it down, such as change the subject, look away, or make light of the matter. Although there are moments when it's reasonable to respond in this way—for example, when we are at work or a social function, we might wait until we get home to let our feelings out—such strategies are problematic when we're not aware of what we're doing. Most often, our defenses become so ingrained that they kick in unconsciously and thus leave us powerless to do things differently. After all, we can't change an unhelpful behavior when we don't even know we're doing it!

Step Two: Taming the Fear

Once you begin to recognize your defenses, you are likely to grow more aware of the underlying discomfort they've been masking.

You might notice your body tensing up, your chest getting tight, or that it's hard to sit still. These and a variety of other somatic experiences (in other words, anything that is felt in your body) are physical manifestations of fear—the fight-or-flight response that's activated when we're feeling threatened. They are also helpful signs that you are getting closer to your feelings.

At the crux of this whole change process is finding a more effective way to deal with your feelings phobia, one that puts you in the driver's seat instead of being unwittingly controlled by fear. I'm going to teach you specific strategies that can help you reduce your discomfort to a much more manageable level so that you no longer need to suppress, dismiss, or try to ignore your feelings. With practice, you'll feel less anxious and be more able to stay present and make room for your emotions.

Step Three: Feeling It Through

Once you begin to notice your feelings and tame your fear, the next step involves letting yourself begin to experience what's inside you. When you fully feel them, feelings have an energetic flow to them. They start small, rise up in a crest, break, and then dissipate—similar to a wave in the ocean. For instance, you might first notice the presence of anger as a niggling sense of frustration. If you tune in to this sensation and give it some space, it then begins to expand. Your body gets warmer, your arms begin to tingle, and you feel an impulse to respond physically. If you stay with this internal experience and don't try to block it or push it away, if you can find a way to ride it out and tolerate it inside you, the feeling of anger peaks and then soon subsides.

Having fully internally ridden out the arc of your feelings, you arrive at a place of energy and clarity where you can reap the many benefits that come from being fully in touch with yourself. You can then freely choose whether or not to take action and, if you do choose to act, how you'd like to proceed and where you want to go. I'm going to teach you healthy ways to experience your feelings and how to manage them effectively so that they don't overwhelm you. You'll develop the skills you need to navigate these new waters and become adept at sailing your emotional ship.

Step Four: Opening Up

The next step brings with it the choice of whether to open up and express what you're feeling inside to others—to put your feelings into words and communicate them—or to keep your feelings to yourself. At times, being in touch with our emotions is enough; we know where we are and what we want to do, and that's all that matters. But more often than not, feelings are meant not just to be experienced but also to be shared. In fact, by getting in touch with your feelings, you'll discover that they also move you to want to open up and reveal them. However, many of us aren't exactly sure how to do this, how to express what we're feeling and how to do it in a way that will maximize our being heard and yield the best results. I'm going to teach you healthy ways to express and share your feelings, how to discriminate between what is wise to express and what is not, and how to use your feelings to get closer and connect more deeply with others. As is true of all these steps, the more you practice revealing your feelings, the easier it will get.

✻

This book is full of stories of transformation. Stories of people like yourself. People who felt stuck, alone, and despairing, but who, in finding the courage to face their fears, in taking the risk to open up to their feelings and share them with others, changed in ways they never imagined possible.

The same can happen for you.

That's precisely what I want you to take away from this book: to know that with the right tools and practice, your life and your relationships can be better.

The capacity for change is there inside you, just waiting to come out. I want to help you harness the amazing wisdom and power of your emotions. You've already taken the first step. You're here with me now. Let's go on this journey together. You'll see: you hold the power within you to transform your life.

Living
LIKE YOU
MEAN IT

PART 1

Preparation

CHAPTER 1

To Feel or Not to Feel

Life shrinks or expands in proportion to one's courage.

—ANAÏS NIN

LISA SLIPPED OUT OF WORK A FEW MINUTES EARLY to get to the airport in time to pick up her boyfriend, Greg. She stopped by the store to get a couple of last-minute things for the special meal she had prepared to welcome him back from his business trip. "That sounds great," Greg said to her as he settled into the front seat a few minutes later. "I should have enough time to eat with you and meet up with the guys later for drinks." Lisa's jaw started to tighten as she thought, *I haven't seen him for how long, and he's planning to see his friends the first night he gets back? Jeez!* She started to stew inside, but hid it behind a cool smile. "So how was your trip?" she asked.

✻

Alex hit the scan button on the car stereo to find something to listen to. It landed on a station playing Christmas carols. "Oh, I love this one, honey, let's listen," his wife said as the familiar melody of "Silent Night" filled the car. Alex felt something catch inside him. It was almost a year to the day that his parents were killed in a car accident on the same road he was now traveling. His mind flooded with holiday memories of his youth, happy times he had spent with his parents. He could feel the tears coming to his eyes and turned his head away from his wife, not wanting her to see. He thought to himself, *Come on, guy, get a hold of yourself. You need to be strong.* He gripped the wheel and struggled to push the feelings down.

✳

Kate had been planning this vacation with her friends for months. Finally, a break after working overtime for far too long. The group got up early and set out on one of the hikes they'd been so looking forward to. As the friends reached the first lookout point, they paused for a moment to take in the view from the mountain. The rising sun cast a gentle orange glow on the arid desert landscape, and the air smelled fresh. *What a perfect day,* Kate thought to herself as she took a deep breath. Suddenly a wave of anxiety came over her, seemingly from nowhere. She turned away, fidgety, unable to be still, and took off up the hill, leaving her bewildered friends behind.

✳

As different as they may seem, these three people are all very much alike. They're afraid of their feelings.

Lisa's afraid of her anger. She holds the anger she feels toward her boyfriend inside. She tries to dismiss it. But as hard as she tries, it eats at her. She ends up feeling resentful, and her anger doesn't go away.

Alex is afraid of his sadness. He's afraid of being vulnerable, of letting his grief over the death of his parents show. He's afraid that if he does, he'll lose all control and become an emotional mess, and his wife will think he's weak.

And Kate is afraid of her happiness. Something about relaxing, enjoying herself, and just being in the moment with her friends makes her anxious, makes her nervous. How sad—to look forward to a vacation for so long and then not be able to really enjoy it.

How sad for all of them, really.

If Lisa felt more comfortable with her anger, if she were able to allow herself to be in touch with it and feel the power of it, maybe she'd have the courage to speak up to her boyfriend, to tell Greg how she feels.

If Alex weren't afraid of his sadness, maybe he'd feel some relief in letting himself grieve more openly for his parents. Maybe he'd share his feelings with his wife, feel closer to her, and not be so alone with his pain. He might even discover—odd as it may seem before the fact—how good it feels to share his pain with another.

And if Kate felt comfortable feeling pleasure with her friends, maybe she'd . . . but wait a minute. Shouldn't it be easy to have feelings that are enjoyable? Yes, it should be, but for many of us it isn't. The vast majority of us experience some degree of discomfort with our feelings, sometimes even the pleasant ones. We start to get close to our emotions, and waves of anxiety stop them dead in their tracks. Or we become fidgety and, rather than feeling what we're feeling, embark on a laundry-folding or house-cleaning marathon instead. We change the subject; distract ourselves with work, television, food; withdraw into silence. We're masters at doing whatever it takes to stay in control.

Simply put, we're *feelings phobic*. We're afraid of our feelings.

A PHOBIA OF SORTS

In psychological terms, a phobia is an exaggerated, inexplicable fear of a particular object or class of objects—spiders, heights, close quarters, and so on. But as Harvard Medical School psychologist Leigh McCullough, PhD, proposed, we can also be afraid of our feelings or emotions, what she called "affect phobia."[1] Someone who is afraid of his or her feelings behaves like Lisa, Alex, and Kate in the stories that opened this chapter.

How would you describe what happens to you when you get close to your feelings? Do you start to feel nervous or uneasy? Or would you describe it as feeling anxious or apprehensive? How about uncomfortable? All these different adjectives have to do with fear. Something is making us want to step back or retreat, and that's how we naturally react to a threat, to something scary. We don't want to have anything to do with it.

With feelings phobia, we want to run from our feelings.

❋

My own struggles with feelings phobia couldn't have been more apparent than on my graduation day from my doctoral program. I had fantasized about this moment for what seemed like an eternity. And there I was, finally about to cross the finish line, about to receive my medal—nothing to do but stop and drink in the sweetness.

As I stood in line waiting for the festivities to begin, I tried to think about all that I had accomplished in the past few years. All the hard work, all the hurdles I had jumped over. I wanted to stop and let myself really savor the moment, to bask in the glory of it all. Hard as I tried, though, I couldn't. I felt agitated and edgy.

I pressed my feet against the floor, forced myself to stand still, and tried to make some space.

A tiny flutter of pride began to come to the surface. *Here we go,* I thought. Just as I was about to make contact with it, a wave of anxiety washed it away.

Damn! What happened? I wondered in dismay. *Let me give it another shot.*

I took a breath and tried to summon up some good feelings, tried to will them into being. Another deep breath, and a slight murmur of happiness sputtered forward. But before I could grab on to it, it was gone, reined in by a strange sense of guilt. As though I didn't deserve to be happy. As though, if I really let myself feel good, something terrible would happen.

This doesn't make sense, I thought. *This is the moment I've been waiting for. I should be thrilled!*

Suddenly a blast of trumpets sounded. My heart quickened as the line in front of me started to move. I walked down the long stretch of the aisle; the cavernous room was filled to capacity with proud parents, relatives, and friends, the air buzzing with anticipation. I scanned the audience for a familiar face, trying to find my family, trying to rise to the occasion. I spotted my two sisters standing in the distance. Their eyes met mine and opened wide with recognition. We smiled and waved with excitement. I could see that they were wiping tears away from their eyes.

Just as I reached my seat, I was suddenly overwhelmed. I started to cry. It was if the floor beneath me were cracking and a giant wave threatened to break through and overtake me. I sat down and braced myself against this torrent of feelings. I pulled myself together and tried to remain very still so that no one would notice the shaking inside me.

What was that about? I wondered. *And why the tears?* Was I moved by the love I saw in my sisters' eyes? By my accomplishments? In part. But these were also tears of pain, tears I didn't understand, tears I couldn't make sense of. So I pushed them away, banishing them to some far-off place.

Later, after managing to get through the ceremony unnoticed, I pasted on a smile and went to find my family. But when I came upon them standing in a group amid the crowd, my mother could see that something was wrong.

"What? What is it, honey?" She asked nervously.

Tears filled my eyes again, and I shook my head. "It's been hard. A lot of work," I offered. I tried to smile, but it was no use. I started crying again, overwhelmed by this deep and confusing sadness.

My family stood there with quizzical looks on their faces. My sister rolled her eyes, my aunt looked perplexed, my father looked away. I felt embarrassed, and looked down, pushed it back, swallowed hard, and tried to act the part of the happy graduate.

On the way home in the car I felt no sense of relief, no satisfaction, certainly no joy. Hardly the delight I had expected. I stared out the window numbly as the buildings passed by in a blur. All I felt was very much alone.

This should have been a joyous moment for me. I should have been filled with pride and a deep sense of satisfaction; grateful for the love of my sisters, my family; happy to the core of my being; and pleased to share these feelings with them. In retrospect, I can see just how powerfully feelings phobia was thwarting my experience, suffocating me and keeping me at a distance. Years and years of stuffed feelings were clogging my system, making it practically impossible for me to be present and to connect, to take in all that was good.

And when the pressure got so intense that these stored-up feelings broke through, they were completely overwhelming and perplexing. I couldn't differentiate one from another.

At the time, I didn't have a clue.

RECOGNIZING THE SIGNS

Most of us are inhibited, to some degree or another, from freely experiencing and expressing our emotions. But many of us aren't aware of what's going on. We might notice feeling fearful, but have no clue about what's causing it: we're too focused on managing our anxiety to be able to see what lies beneath. More often than not, though, we're so cut off that we're barely aware that we're even uncomfortable at all. The full extent of our distress is hidden just outside our awareness, lurking behind the scenes, but controlling our every move. We're so disconnected, so adept at avoiding our emotions, we don't even see what's going on. We don't see how masterful we've become at shutting off our feelings before they even get started. In fact, we've gotten so good at steering clear of our emotions, we're not even aware that there are feelings inside us at all! Although the first step to my four-step approach is *becoming aware* of your feelings and the specific defenses you use to avoid them, let's begin by first doing a bit of consciousness raising about our general relationship with our feelings.

Are You Afraid of Your Feelings?

Even though you may not be aware of being uncomfortable with emotion or what's going on behind the scenes, with a little thought you can uncover the signs of feelings phobia. Take a moment now to stop and consider how you react to your feelings. These lists of the common signs of feelings phobia are not meant to be exhaustive, but they should help you begin to get a good idea of just how comfortable you are with your emotions.

Afraid of Feelings in General

- Avoiding situations that might be emotional (for example, visiting a grieving or sick friend, saying good-bye to coworkers when

leaving a job, being acknowledged for an accomplishment, addressing a conflict or disappointment with a loved one)
- Smiling or laughing when you're actually feeling something else (such as sadness, anger, or fear)
- Finding it difficult to be still and stay present with yourself
- Overthinking what you want to do, turning thoughts over and over in your head and not being able to take action
- Perpetually complaining about a situation, but not doing anything to change it
- Always needing to be in control
- When faced with questions about your emotions, feeling at a loss to identify how you feel

Afraid of Being Emotionally Close or Intimate with Others

- Physically turning away from others when any emotion starts to stir inside you, perhaps even with people you feel close to
- Feeling discomfort or nervousness with sharing a silent moment with someone
- Feeling embarrassed or ashamed for feeling a particular way
- Feeling uncomfortable with prolonged eye contact
- Getting anxious when someone else expresses his or her feelings
- Not being able to acknowledge or openly express what you feel inside

Uncomfortable with and Avoiding Sadness or Grief

- Not wanting to cry in front of anyone, holding back tears
- Feeling afraid of being or seeming vulnerable, not wanting to appear weak, acting as if you're unaffected
- Worrying that you won't be able to stop crying, that you'll lose control or go crazy

Afraid of Anger or Assertiveness

- Never allowing yourself to get angry
- Stewing over something and feeling resentful for a long time

- Avoiding angry feelings until it's too late, and they end up coming out in a messy explosion or temper tantrum
- Expressing your anger by being passive (for example, showing up late, not returning a phone call, "forgetting" to do something) instead of being direct
- Having difficulty standing up for yourself or voicing a position that's different from others'
- Feeling obligated to be nice or good, but feeling resentful inside and then accusing yourself of being a bad person

Afraid of Happiness or Pleasure

- Not being able to feel a real sense of pleasure or joy for very long
- Dismissing your accomplishments or putting off the good feelings to a later time
- Not being able to share a sense of pride or happiness with others
- Feeling uncomfortable accepting compliments and praise from others
- Having difficulty being spontaneous

A Matter of Degree

Do any of these signs seem familiar to you? Maybe you identified with several of them, or perhaps with only a few. That's because the degree to which we're afraid of our feelings can vary. It all hinges on just how much anxiety or fear we experience when we get close to our feelings.

Some people are afraid of having any feelings at all. Their fear is so strong that they completely clamp down on what's going on inside them, obliterating any possibility of allowing their feelings to come to the surface. But if you look closely at these people, you might be surprised. Although they may seem emotionless, more often than not they're incredibly anxious. And somewhere beneath all their anxiety, outside their awareness, are feelings. They're just too uncomfortable even to see that there are feelings there.

On the other end of the spectrum are people who are highly emotional and unable to consistently modulate and make their feelings work for them. Their challenge is not to open up to their feelings but to find a way to turn the dial down and regulate their emotional experience. Although some of the techniques I'm going to share with you could be helpful to people who struggle in this way, this book is primarily intended for those of us who need help to be more fully in touch with our feelings.

Most of us seem to be more comfortable with certain feelings and less so with others. For instance, you may be someone who has an easy time letting your hair down and laughing with friends, but have a difficult time with feelings of anger. Or you might not have a problem being angry, but are very uncomfortable with the "softer" feelings, such as sadness, tenderness, and closeness. Or you might be fine with feeling sad, but don't feel comfortable with taking the time to enjoy yourself, to feel satisfied, or to feel a sense of pride in your accomplishments.

Here, though, is a case of things not always being as they seem. When we have difficulty experiencing one particular feeling, our ability to be really comfortable with other feelings is hampered as well. When we suppress even one feeling, they are all affected. Our discomfort with anger affects our experience of joy; our fear of sadness affects our experience of love. And so on, and so on, and so on.

Take Lisa, whom we met earlier.

It's All Connected

When Lisa first came to see me, she described herself as normally "happy-go-lucky," able to enjoy herself, laugh, and have a good time. As far as she was concerned, the cause of her frustration and dismay was her boyfriend. If Greg wasn't so selfish and insensitive to her feelings, she wouldn't be feeling so unhappy. Right?

Well, possibly.

There's no doubt that it would help if Greg were more attuned to Lisa. But Lisa's inability to experience and deal with her anger is also a problem.

When Lisa avoids and stuffs down her anger, she's left feeling resentful and annoyed, and these feelings permeate her life.

She feels disconnected from Greg, is distracted when they're together, doesn't fully enjoy being with him, and has lost interest in having sex. Moreover, she feels depressed; she's not happy at work and has little energy for things she used to enjoy doing. All these different aspects of her life are affected by her inability to deal with her anger. It's as though there's no room for any other feelings as long as that unresolved anger is still inside her.

When Lisa and I got to work on her feelings phobia, she was eventually able to overcome her fear and accept and handle her emotions. We started by helping Lisa develop emotional mindfulness. She needed to become aware that underneath her actions, she was actually quite angry with Greg. This is step one in the four-part process: *becoming aware*. In addition, I helped Lisa identify the ways in which she had been avoiding her anger. She began to recognize her tendency to dismiss her feelings, rationalize them away ("I'm just tired," "I'm being too hard on Greg," and so on), and try to stuff or swallow her anger. Next, I helped Lisa learn how to ease the discomfort she felt when she would get close to her feelings. This is the second part of the process, what I've called *taming the fear*. She learned how to tune in to the tension she felt in her body, relax her muscles, and breathe into her experience. With practice, she was able to safely open up to an internal experience of her anger—the third step, *feeling it through*—and then make use of the positive energy she discovered in its wake. Once Lisa became more adept at handling her feelings and sharing them with Greg—in the fourth step, *opening up*—she experienced improvement not only in her relationship with him but also in all the other areas of her life. She felt happy, was enthusiastic about her job, and felt a renewed sense of energy for life. As she described it, she felt as if "an essential life force had returned."

As we neared the end of our work together, Lisa shared this experience with me.

She and Greg had recently gone away for the weekend to have some alone time. They drove out to a resort in the mountains after work one Friday, arrived late in the evening bleary-eyed, and collapsed into bed, relieved to have a few days off after a long, hard workweek.

The next morning, they awoke to the sun streaming into the room. Lisa got out of bed and pulled the curtain aside. The view was magnificent. The morning sun danced on the lake, and the majestic pine trees seemed to touch the sky.

"Greg, you have to see this," she said.

He ambled over to the window and put his arm around her. "Man, how beautiful!" he said.

They stood together in silence, holding each other, the hassles of the workweek gradually melting away. *This is just what we needed,* Lisa thought to herself as a warm glow came over her.

After breakfast, Lisa ran back to the room to get her camera. As she stepped off the elevator into the lobby, she could see Greg in the distance on his cell phone, pacing back and forth.

Something stirred inside her. *He must be talking to someone about work,* she thought, and started to feel irritated. *We had agreed to let go of work for the weekend.* Greg spotted her and quickly got off the phone.

"Who was that?" Lisa asked him as she approached him.

"Oh, no one, just checking my messages. Come on, let's get going."

As they headed out to the trail, Lisa could tell that Greg was distracted, clearly wrapped up in thinking about some work issue. She felt a burning sensation growing inside her, which she now understood to be her anger. For a moment, she thought of letting it go. But then she caught herself.

"I knew where that would lead," she said to me with a smile. "I would have been fuming the whole weekend." Instead, she tried something different.

"Greg," she said to him. "I'm feeling angry. We had agreed to put work behind us for the weekend."

"I wasn't talking to anyone. I was just checking my messages," he said defensively.

Lisa felt the anger rise up in her again, but stayed the course.

"It doesn't matter whether you were checking your messages or talking to someone," she asserted. "Now you're thinking about work. Now you're distracted, and it's affecting our time together."

Greg looked away and was quiet for a moment. He seemed to be wrestling with something inside him. Then he sighed, looked back at Lisa, and said earnestly, "You're right. I'm sorry. It's just so hard for me to let go sometimes."

She could see the regret in his eyes and felt the anger inside her ebb. A sense of relief quickly replaced it. *Wow, this is different,* she thought to herself, and felt the warmth inside her return. They took each other's hand and started off on a walk together.

Lisa looked at me, her eyes moist. It wasn't sadness. No. She was moved.

"We had a really great weekend," she said. "I felt so close to Greg."

"How was that?" I asked.

"Wonderful," she said.

I looked over at her, sitting up straight, looking pleased and proud of herself for the way she handled that moment with Greg—for all the work she had done to now be able to express herself.

"Yes, this certainly *is* different," I said to her, and we shared a smile of deep understanding.

✳

That's what it can be like for people who are more able to be with and share their feelings. They have a healthy sense of self; they are able to be assertive and get their needs met, feel pride in their accomplishments, and experience deep moments of joy. They're able to cry when sad, grieve when there's a loss, and feel the fire of anger when threatened or attacked. They enjoy being close with others; are able to experience warm, loving feelings; and can make love with abandon.

Sounds great, doesn't it?

Why Bother?

Maybe not. Maybe you still have doubts. Maybe you've come along for the ride so far, but there's a part of you thinking, *Don't our feelings just get in the way? They're so irrational! Don't they just make things worse? Mess things up? Won't I just end up wallowing in them? Wouldn't it be better if I didn't have to deal with my feelings, if I could just rely on my thinking to get me through?*

If you're asking yourself questions like these, I'm not surprised. They're common beliefs; many of my clients say the same things when they first come to see me. When I initially encourage them to explore their emotions, they ask me "What good will that do?" or "Where will that get me?" Often my response is this: "How has *not* paying attention to your feelings worked for you so far?"

If avoiding your feelings is working fine for you, stop reading. Keep doing what you're doing. Don't mess with it if it's not broken, right?

Chances are, however, that if you chose to pick up this book, avoiding your feelings is not working, and you're stuck. You'd like to move forward, but you also have some reasonable questions.

So let me take a moment to address some of your concerns.

The Old "Make Things Worse, Mess Things Up, Get in the Way" Argument It's not your feelings that make things worse; it's what you do to try to deny them or make them go away that's causing you problems.

Of course there are times when you may need to modulate your feelings, to hold them in and not act on them, depending on the situation you're in. But, in general, when you try to cut your feelings off even to the extent that you don't allow yourself to experience them inside you, you're working against a natural process. As humans, we're *wired* to feel and to connect emotionally. Our feelings are actually a part of our neurobiological make-up— they're signals sent from our brain in direct response to something in our environment. When you try to ignore your feelings, push them down, or hold them back, you're short-circuiting an innate process, one that was designed with your best interests in mind.

Think about it from an evolutionary perspective. Emotions played a key role in ensuring our survival as a species. Prehistoric humans wouldn't have lasted very long in the wilderness if they had had no emotional reaction to a ferocious animal charging toward them. It was the emotion of fear that got their hearts pumping faster, caused the blood to rush to their legs, and prompted them to run. Nor would they have lasted very long without close emotional bonds with others, which helped them feel safe and protected so that they could prevail despite enormous challenges.

Quite simply, our emotions developed and endured over millions of years because they're essential to our existence.

Think about the significant ways in which our feelings help us in our lives today.

Excitement and joy encourage us to open up, get involved, or stay engaged in activities that already have our interest. Love urges us to move closer, to be nearer to a loved one, to open up and share more deeply. Anger motivates us to protect or defend ourselves, set boundaries or limits when necessary, raise our voices and be heard. Disgust prompts us to pull back, turn away, and avoid something that may be potentially harmful. Grief and sadness alike prompt us to slow down, to take the time to address whatever is making us sad—losses, disappointments, hurts—to cry and talk about our pain, to seek solace from others, to do what we need to do to take care of ourselves, let go, and move on.

Aren't these all healthy things?

In this very basic way, our emotions mobilize and guide us to deal with life and the different situations that come our way in a positive, life-enhancing manner. As neuroscientist Joseph LeDoux wrote, "[Emotions] chart the course of moment-to-moment action as well as set the sails toward long-term achievements."[2] And they help us communicate what is going on inside us and adaptively connect with others.

Feelings, when dealt with in a healthy way, don't make things worse, they make things *better.*

Wallowing in Feelings Like Alex, who was afraid to mourn his dead parents, you may worry that opening yourself up to your feelings may cause you to wallow in them. But, plain and simple, wallowing is not *feeling* our feelings. Wallowing is what happens when we're stuck. It's what happens when we're *not* feeling our feelings all the way through to completion, when we're not going with the energetic flow of our emotions and with where they're wired to take us.

When Alex told me he was worried that he'd "just end up wallowing" in his sorrow, I seized the opportunity to address this common misperception that feelings are never-ending (which, by the way, is a typical defense against sadness). I explained, "All feelings have a natural flow to them. Like a wave, they rise up, crescendo, then dissipate. When feelings are fully felt, they really don't last very long—sometimes minutes, sometimes only seconds."

"Really?" Alex looked at me with some disbelief, but I could see the wheels turning.

I told him, "It's only when the natural flow of our feelings is thwarted—often by fear, anxiety, or depression, when we get defensive, or when we don't have the support we might need to face something overwhelming—that we become caught in this in-between place, not going fully in one direction or another. Really feeling our emotions is what puts an end to wallowing and allows us to move forward."

He nodded with recognition, and tears came to his eyes, a sign that he was beginning to allow his feelings to run their natural course

❋

It's not that it wasn't scary for Alex to open up to his feelings after that, or that my words radically shifted things for him. Still, knowing that his sadness wouldn't last forever and that there was actually something good that came from the process allowed Alex to feel a little less anxious and more able to begin to move in a healthy direction. Taking one's fears out and holding them up to the light of reality can often help reduce them. We'll talk more about how to address your anxiety and fears in Chapter Five, "Taming the Fear."

Not surprisingly, beneath Alex's fear was, among other feelings, a deep well of grief. Grief not just about losing his parents but also about the lack of closeness he experienced with them when they were alive. As we began to examine his feelings, Alex became increasingly aware of just how much emotion he had been avoiding. To make the process more manageable and not so overwhelming, we spent some time clarifying and disentangling the different feelings Alex had—sadness, anger, guilt, and love—and mindfully giving each some room to breathe. With each emotional experience Alex allowed himself to have, he also experienced a deep sense of relief and renewal. He found himself feeling more alive, more connected to himself, and more connected to others in his life. And he stopped worrying so much about wallowing.

Better to Rely on Thinking? The rational mind—having the ability to think things through and exercise reason—is a good and necessary thing. But for a long time, thinking was seen as the be-all and end-all to our mental health. Now we know better. Now we know that our *emotional* mind also plays a fundamental role in our well-being.

Think about it for a moment. If our rational mind were so powerful, how is it that our feelings are often able to override our thinking? How is it that we can know one thing intellectually— such as, "there's nothing to be afraid of"—but our feelings can convince us otherwise?

Take Kate. She had been dreaming about her vacation for months, but now that it's finally here, she can't enjoy herself. She's overcome with anxiety, feels guilty about enjoying herself, worries that if she does let go and have a little fun something bad might happen.

Kate's worries are irrational. She's fully aware that she has the time off coming to her. She knows there's nothing wrong with enjoying oneself. And she knows that even if something bad did happen, she could handle it. Yet her worries and fears keep overpowering her thoughts.

Clearly there's something more going on below the surface for Kate, but why isn't she able to get on top of it? Why can't she just be rational about it and refute her feelings with reason?

Part of the answer lies in how our brain operates.

Recall what I said in the Introduction about how feelings can be more powerful than thoughts? In recent years, technological advances have enabled scientists to understand more precisely just how the brain functions. Joseph LeDoux, in his fascinating book *The Emotional Brain,* clearly illustrates how the neural connections that run from the emotional parts of the brain to the thinking parts of the brain are actually much stronger and more numerous than the connections that run in the other direction.[3] This helps explain why at times emotions are able to overwhelm our thoughts and dominate our thinking and why it can be difficult to control strong emotions through rational thought alone.

Sometimes, trying to dictate our feelings with thinking is like trying to swim against the current. We'd be better off learning how to accept and work with our feelings rather than in fighting the tide.

The Valuable Information We Get from Our Feelings

Here's a little test: imagine trying to make a decision without your feelings to guide you. Try to decide where you would like your life to be in five years. How about ten years? Think about what it would be like to choose a partner or spouse without consulting your feelings. Go ahead. Give it a try. It's practically impossible. Without our feelings, we have no idea of how we'll be affected by our decisions once we make them.

This is one of the reasons those of us with feelings phobia end up making bad decisions or end up staying stuck in relationships or situations that are not good for us. We're too afraid to listen to and trust the feelings inside us, to trust that gut sense we get. Of course, relying solely on our emotions to make a decision without acknowledging relevant data can also be a problem. The trick is to be able to consult with our feelings and use them to guide us, while also incorporating other helpful information into our process. If we could find the courage to truly be with our feelings, to pay attention to them and heed what they're telling us, we would probably have a clearer understanding of what we should do. We might also discover the motivation and energy we need to move forward and make a change.

TO BE OR NOT TO BE

Your personal identity—the core of who you are—is largely formed by what you feel and how you react. Your likes and dislikes, what makes you happy, what makes you sad, what excites you, what brings you pleasure, what annoys you, what frustrates you or gets your blood boiling—all say so much about who you are as a person.

It's in our feelings that we find our true authentic self. When we avoid or deny our feelings, when we suppress them, we are in a way denying who we are, squelching our individual voice and sacrificing our true potential and power.

❄

Have you ever heard a song a hundred times over and then one day, seemingly out of the blue, it speaks to you in a totally different way? This very thing happened to me at a difficult time in my life, a time in which I was painfully struggling to figure out whether the five-year relationship I had been in was really right for me.

I was getting ready for work one morning, going about my usual routine, and I popped a CD in the stereo to liven things up a bit. As I brushed my teeth, "Meadowlark," a song by Stephen Schwartz from the musical *The Baker's Wife,* started to play. I had heard it many times before and had always loved it. This time, however, the words caught my attention, strangely resonant, and drew me in.

This woman sang the story of a bird, a meadowlark who had a beautiful, angelic voice but was unable to see. One day, the meadowlark is discovered by an old king, who brings her to his castle, showers her with riches, and promises to take care of her for the rest of her life; all she has to do in return is sing for him. Sounds like a good deal. So she agrees and is content for quite some time.

Then one day, while the meadowlark was singing by the river, the God of the Sun chances upon her, hears her singing, and is so taken by her beautiful voice that he grants her the gift of sight. When she opens her eyes, she beholds him, a beautiful young man, standing there before her. He asks her to fly with him to the ends of the earth and live a life filled with all that she's secretly longed for.

She wants to go with him in the worst way, to live the life she has so yearned to live, a life that she had denied herself. But she can't bring herself to do it. She's afraid. Afraid of hurting the old king. Afraid to spread her wings and fly. Afraid to be true to her feelings. She can't bear the thought of it, so she declines.

Disappointed, the sun god says good-bye and flies away. Later that day, when the king comes looking for the meadowlark, he finds her lifeless on the ground. Dead.

At that moment in the song, something unlocked inside me. I was struck by the most profound realization. I started to cry, a crying that quickly turned to sobbing. Unearthed from somewhere deep inside me, this tremendous grief burst forward through the dam, coming forth in waves, one after the other.

Unlike my graduation day, this time I knew what I was crying about.

I was the meadowlark! Her story was my story. I had become so afraid of following my heart, of going with and trusting my feelings, that I had unknowingly cut off an essential part of me—a vital, deep-feeling core that knew what I wanted, what I longed for, what felt right and what felt wrong to me—my truest self. It had been trapped inside me, bound up by fear. Lost. Lost for so long.

But not anymore. I could hear my true voice now, and I couldn't let myself end up like the meadowlark. I knew what I needed to do. I knew that I had to leave the relationship I was in and move on. It wasn't easy. No, in fact, it was one of the hardest things I've ever done. It felt challenging and scary at times, but deep down inside me it felt right. I couldn't sacrifice myself any longer. I needed to listen to my heart.

It takes courage to allow yourself to feel and to let your feelings guide you through your everyday life. By cutting those bonds that keep you locked up inside, you allow your feelings to soar, to be fully felt. So you can soar as well. You can give yourself the gift of your true potential rather than imprisoning your feelings—and yourself—like the lifeless meadowlark.

❄

The next chapter says more about how and why we imprison ourselves every day. Understanding why we're held back is an important step for those of us who want ultimately to be able to experience and share our feelings and ourselves in a full and expansive way. To feel alive and vital, to feel more deeply connected to our loved ones, and to enjoy the richness, fulfillment, and contentedness that come from a life openly felt and lived.

You are already on your way to becoming more aware of and attuned to the emotions inside you. You are on your way to getting to know yourself.

CHAPTER TAKE-HOME POINTS

- Feelings are a part of our natural make-up and, as such, are a "wired-in" response.
- Our emotions are there for our benefit.
- It's in our feelings that we find our true, authentic self.
- Most people, to some degree or another, are afraid of their feelings. This kind of fear can be called a feelings phobia.
- Our defenses, not our feelings themselves, can cause us to get stuck.
- Suppressed feelings can lead to a wide range of physical, emotional, and psychological problems.
- Feelings are like waves and have a natural flow to them. They rise up, crescendo, and then dissipate.
- Our brain is wired such that our emotions are stronger and operate much faster than thoughts.
- Feelings are an essential guide in decision making.
- The core of your being is formed by what and how you feel. When you avoid your feelings, you're squelching your identity and thwarting your true potential.
- Although it takes courage to face your feelings, the rewards are numerous.

CHAPTER 2

How the Heck Did I Get This Way?

History, despite its wrenching pain, cannot be unlived,
but if faced with courage, need not be lived again.
—MAYA ANGELOU

KAREN HAD BEEN TALKING FOR NEARLY FIFTEEN MINUTES about the various problems she was having with her husband, yet I still wasn't sure how she really felt. The difficulties that had been mounting over the last five years had driven her to the end of her rope. At least that's what she said. But that wasn't quite what I was seeing. As she sat across from me, fashionably dressed, with dark straight hair and wide brown eyes, telling me about her painful experiences, she was smiling.

What am I supposed to make of this smile? I wondered. *It seems out of place. Is it a nervous smile? Is she feeling embarrassed? Is she worried what I might think?* The look on her face, childlike in a way, was a mask that hid her true feelings. It reminded me of a time when my own anxiety had become so strong that it was like a wall, a formidable fortress that not only kept others out but also kept me from my own feelings.

What's behind Karen's smile? I thought. *What is she unknowingly working so hard to cover up?*

"Karen, can I ask you what you're feeling right now? You've been telling me about all these painful things going on for you, but all the while you've been mostly smiling. I'm not sure what's going on for you in terms of your feelings."

Karen paused for a brief second and then took a stab at it. "I don't know," she said. "I mean, I guess I'm upset."

I wasn't surprised that she didn't know how she felt. It seemed to me that she hadn't made contact with her feelings—hadn't yet become more emotionally mindful.

"Well, take a moment and check in with yourself," I suggested. "What are you noticing right now inside you?"

Her smile began to melt as she dipped below the surface for the first time since sitting down. "Um, I feel a little tense. A little nervous, I guess."

"Where in your body do you notice that?" I hoped that becoming more aware of her bodily experience would help her get closer to her feelings.

Her hand slid up to her chest. "Right here . . . it feels tight."

"Just notice that," I encouraged.

As she did, her eyes filled up with tears. Then, in a small, tentative voice, she said, "Actually, I think I'm feeling a little afraid."

"Really? Of what?" I asked, as gently as I could.

"I don't know. I guess about what you might be thinking." She paused for a moment and then continued. "It's weird. I feel small all of a sudden. Like a little girl. And I'm afraid. I'm afraid that you're going to think I'm bad. That I'm bad for feeling this way. That I'm bad for having my feelings."

Karen and I soon discovered that she often felt this way about her feelings, and not just with me. She was frequently uncomfortable feeling and trusting her emotions and wondered if she was crazy for feeling the way she did.

WHAT WENT WRONG?

What caused Karen to approach her emotions with such uncertainty? To feel that she's bad? Why does she expect that others will respond to her feelings with disapproval? How is it that Karen became so uncomfortable with really feeling, believing, and sharing her feelings? For that matter, how is it that so many of us become this way—become afraid of our feelings?

We certainly don't start out in the world afraid.

Perhaps you have children of your own, or family or friends who have a baby. Take a moment and think about what babies are like when it comes to having feelings. Have you noticed how their emotions just flow? Whenever I'm in the presence of infants, I'm struck by how free they can be with their feelings. They smile and laugh when they're happy, cry when discontent, get angry when frustrated in some way; they readily express and communicate basic emotions. So much life. Such vitality. It's such a delight to witness, the richness of human experience so naturally and easily present.

Yet these fully feeling wonders stand in stark contrast to Karen and to so many adults whom I encounter both professionally and personally. Now, I'm not suggesting that we should behave as infants do and not modulate our feelings in any way. That, of course, would not be healthy. We need to be able to handle our feelings in an adult, mature manner. But if we were born emotionally uninhibited, what happens to us that causes us to become so constricted? How do we lose this ability to be in touch and so free?

The answer can be found by looking at our earliest emotional experiences.

IN THE BEGINNING

Although everyone is born with the ability to have feelings, as infants we don't know what to do with them. We're not quite sure how to handle or make sense of them. In this very basic way, we're utterly dependent on our caregivers to teach us how to navigate this new world of emotions.

We need our caregivers to be attuned to us and respond to our feelings, to validate them and help us understand their worth. We need them to help us cope with and manage our emotions, such as anger, sadness, and the need for closeness, especially when these feelings are intense or overwhelming. When caregivers help babies and young children regulate emotions successfully (for example, rubbing a scared child's back while reassuring her of being safe; talking with a young child about his anger and helping him develop constructive ways to express it, as well as dealing with the situation that evoked the anger to begin with; and so on), children develop the ability to feel and experience their feelings fully and to express and deal with them in a healthy way. And the broader the range of feelings we experience as children, the larger and more flexible our emotional range will be as we grow and develop.[1]

When our caregivers are emotionally open, when they're comfortable with and skilled at attending to feelings, this whole enterprise goes off without a hitch, and we become emotionally competent ourselves. But therein lies the rub. Many caregivers don't have these qualities. Many of us grew up with parents who were more or less uncomfortable with emotions—their own and those of others. In fact, some of us grew up with parents who were feelings phobic.

This is precisely why and how things go awry.

Attachment studies and infant development research have shown that as babies we're extremely sensitive to the cues we receive about feelings from our caregivers. When our parents are uncomfortable with certain feelings and when they react negatively to them, even subtly, we pick up on this. We keenly sense and learn from our earliest experiences which feelings are acceptable and which aren't. We're able to recognize which feelings make our parents uncomfortable and which bring them pleasure, which ones draw them close and which ones cause them to pull away. And, as psychologist Diana Fosha explains in her book *The Transforming Power of Affect,* to preserve our primary attachment relationships, we adjust our emotional repertoire accordingly by suppressing the feelings that threaten our sense of safety and security.[2] We do whatever it takes to keep Mommy close or to please Daddy. For example:

- A child playing with his toys gets frustrated and angry when one rolls out of reach. His mother gets anxious at this display and freezes up. The child senses her distress and, over time, learns to restrict his anger.
- An infant gets excited, waving her arms, kicking her legs, and squealing in delight. Her father withdraws abruptly, hoping

she'll calm down. The child senses the distance and, over time, learns to curb her excitement.

- A little boy is frightened and cries when the neighbor's dog barks at him. His father reacts with irritation and disdain. Over time, the child learns to suppress vulnerable feelings like fear and sadness.
- Exuberant, a little girl runs into the house from playing and goes to shower her mother with hugs and kisses. Her mother recoils and says, "Don't be silly." The child eventually learns to restrain her love and affection and hide her need for closeness and comfort.
- A little boy, overwhelmed by his father's demands, retaliates in anger saying, "I hate you!" His father, unable to deal with his son's anger at him, emotionally and physically withdraws and does not speak to his son for several days. This child learns to fear his anger and to feel guilty for asserting himself.

Isolated moments such as these may not have long-lasting effects, especially if the parent repairs the disruption with attunement and connection—in other words, reaches out and communicates. But repeated experiences along these lines cause children to suppress and deny the feelings that are likely to cause a negative reaction from their caregivers.

Our suppressing problematic emotions as children is adaptive, as it helps us get our primary needs for safety and security met and allows us to maintain a connection to our primary caregivers, but it has a high cost: it compromises our inborn ability to feel and express our feelings. Our development as emotional beings is thwarted, and our emotional capacity is constricted. We end up cut off from our emotional self and cut off from others.

I AM A ROCK, I AM AN ISLAND

Behind Karen's smile was a host of feelings. Profound pain, sadness, grief, and a good deal of anger—to name just a few. Feelings she had dutifully learned to push down and hide. Feelings that had no place in her house when she was growing up. As I worked with Karen to help her face and decrease the fear that made her feel like a little girl, she told me about what life was like for her when she was a child. In particular, life with her mother.

Karen's mother was emotionally unpredictable; Karen never knew what kind of mood her mother would be in or when it might suddenly turn sour. Although sometimes pleasant, her mother could also be irritable and even volatile at times. This "hot-and-cold" disposition pervaded the house and kept the rest of the family on edge, tiptoeing around her, doing all they could to avoid what Karen described as "one of Mom's violent pouts." Karen's father tried everything he could to appease his wife and keep her happy, but the results were at best only short lived.

Karen's mother was especially critical of Karen and would frequently yell at her for little or no apparent reason. On one particular occasion, Karen recalled coming home from school on a snowy winter day, excited that the girls in the neighborhood had asked her to come out and play. Her mother, unable to step outside her own emotional angst and embrace her daughter's joy, lowered the boom. "If I have to stay inside and not have any fun, then so do you!"

Parenthetically, unbeknownst to anyone until very recently, Karen's mother was a survivor of rape. This tragic incident occurred when she was in her late teens and resulted in a child whom she gave up for adoption. Her mother kept these traumatic experiences secret, tried to put them behind her, tried to extinguish the emotional pain she suffered, but she clearly continued to be distressed on some level—a testament to the toxic effects of pushing down one's feelings. One can only imagine how this unresolved trauma played a part in Karen's mother's mercurial moods.

Karen's strategy for dealing with her mother's erratic behavior was to try to be the best little girl that she could—always smiling, obedient, and self-reliant. In a fundamental way, she learned to dismiss her own emotional needs and stuff down any feelings that might make her mother uncomfortable, engender disdain, or set her off. Although often rewarded for her efforts to please, Karen was also admonished for not trying hard enough and was left with the sense that she could always do better. Underneath it all she was suffering, longing to be cared for, comforted, and embraced in a whole and unconditional way.

This "smile-and-tough-it-out" approach made a lot of sense at the time. It was a valid way to cope with an untenable situation and helped Karen get through her early years in her family as best she could. Over time, this pattern of pleasing others and neglecting her own feelings became her standard way of responding and, as such, left her disconnected from her emotional experience as well as from those she was closest to, including her husband. What had helped her maintain a connection with her mother as a child had now become a liability. As I helped Karen become more emotionally mindful, she began to see how she avoided her feelings and how she had in a way become a master at denial. In fact, she told me that her husband had once described her as being like "an island" emotionally.

IT'S ALL IN YOUR HEAD

You might be thinking, *Karen's an adult now; she doesn't need to worry about her mother's moods anymore. She's free to have her feelings and be her own person.* There's some truth to this line of thought. Karen *is* an adult, and she should be free to be her own person. The problem is that her brain is operating on old programming and will continue to operate in this way until she's able to "rewire" herself by overcoming her fear and experiencing something new and different—by facing and dealing with her feelings.

To make sense of these physiological dynamics in all of us, it helps to have a bit of an understanding about how the brain develops and works. The brain itself is made up of several different regions, each with its own particular function. For instance, one area of the brain makes sense of what we see, another area assesses whether we're in danger, another oversees the performance of motor skills, and so on. Within these different areas of the brain are millions of nerve cells that communicate to one another by sending messages across the synapses, the small gaps between them. The pathways that form between nerve cells make up the "wiring" of the brain and are what enable the different regions of the brain to communicate and work together in harmony.[3]

At birth, most of the one hundred billion neurons in the brain are not yet connected into networks. Brain growth is actually the result of an ever-unfolding process that involves the wiring and rewiring of neural connections. What then, you may be wondering, determines how our brain gets wired? We used to believe that brain development was largely governed by genetics, but as UCLA psychiatrist Daniel Siegel explains in his book *The Developing Mind*, we now understand that it has very much to do with experience.[4]

THE ROAD MORE TRAVELED

Imagine going for a walk in the woods. As you make your way through the forest, it's likely that you've chosen to stay on a well-worn path rather than try to establish a new trail. At some point in time, though, the path that is guiding your way was not there. Some determined soul forged that trail, and over time others followed in his footsteps. Now it's become the easiest road to travel, and you don't think twice about letting it lead the way.

This scenario illustrates in simplified form how neural pathways are created in the brain. An initial experience lays down a trail between nerve cells. The more this same experience is repeated, the stronger and more defined the pathway becomes. Eventually, it becomes so deeply etched into the landscape of our brain that it becomes the automatic route on which signals travel. Our brain requires stimulation to grow and mature optimally. In particular, it needs the kind of stimulation that comes through interacting and engaging with others. Early relational experiences with our parents or caregivers play a significant role in determining how our brain is shaped and formed, how it is wired.

Let's think about this process in respect to our emotional development. Although it takes a little over two decades for the brain to mature fully, the first two years of life are a critical period in which the brain develops at an astonishing rate. During this time, the experiences that shape our brain are largely based in the *emotion* that arises in interaction with the important people in our life.[5]

Again, recall your personal experience of being with an infant. As babies, we're not able to speak: we have no words, no language to convey our needs and wants. Everything is communicated through the "language" of the face, the eyes, the body; through touch, sounds, vocal tone and rhythms. Everything is communicated through feelings rather than through words. We let those around us know what is going on inside us by expressing our feelings. We're born with the capacity to feel and express a few basic emotions. Fairly rapidly, our emotional repertoire expands. Within the first six months of life, we're able to experience joy, sadness, disgust, and anger; by eight months, fear. With each successive year, our emotional capacity grows and becomes more complex. By two to three years of age, we're also able to feel pride, embarrassment, shame, and guilt.[6]

Our early emotional exchanges with our parents profoundly affect the workings of our brain and, consequently, how we experience our feelings. If our caregivers favorably respond to our emotional expression—that is, in an attuned, accepting, and encouraging way—then we come to associate our feelings with a positive sense of being. For instance, recall the example I mentioned earlier of the little boy who angrily said to his father, "I hate you!" If, instead of withdrawing and not talking to his son for several days, the father were able to remain connected and be responsive, tolerate the outburst, stay open, inquire about what was making his son so angry, and help the child find another way to express himself, the child's experience would be positive and productive. He would learn to manage and deal with his anger, become more facile at expressing himself in an adaptive way, and come to associate his feelings with a positive outcome.

If instead our emotions are responded to in a way that causes us to feel anxious or afraid, they become linked in our memory with a sense of danger. For example, many parents feel conflicted and disturbed when a child gets angry and says, "I hate you." In return they might become irritated, enraged, or dejected and react with disdain, contempt, or depression. Further, they might punish or shame the child or, as in the example here, make him feel guilty by withdrawing.

Good or bad, the more a particular interaction is repeated during childhood, the stronger these associations and the related neural pathways become. Eventually, depending on our experiences, either confidence or fear becomes burned into our brain's circuitry as an automatic response to any or all of our feelings. These emotional lessons have a significant impact on how we experience ourselves, others, and the world.

The effects of this hardwiring are powerful and long lasting.

KAREN'S BRAIN

Although Karen's memory of her childhood gives us a good idea of why she's afraid of her feelings, the groundwork for her fear was probably set in place even earlier than what she remembers.

Let's imagine what life might have been like for Karen when she was a baby. Given what we know about Karen's mother, it's safe to assume that she was depressed around the time that her daughter was born, and the stress of having and caring for a tiny baby pushed her to her limits. In addition, Karen's mother brought to this experience her own emotional limitations. When Karen cried or fussed, as babies so often do, her mother may have felt overwhelmed; she may have reacted with discomfort or pulled away. Maybe she got frustrated or angry with her. Perhaps she was even shaming.

From a baby's perspective, these responses are quite scary. They carry with them the threat of reprimand, rejection, and, ultimately—the biggest fear of all—abandonment (which to an infant is the equivalent of death). As research into early attachment relationships has shown, our needs for safety, security, and closeness are biologically based and trump all others—they're essential to our survival.[7]

So, in a very basic way, Karen learned that having certain feelings was treacherous. *If I'm sad, Mommy leaves me. If I'm upset, Mommy gets angry.* What was she to do to cope with such a difficult situation? Aware of these negative reactions, and geared to do whatever she needed to do to survive, Karen adjusted her behavior accordingly—to keep her mother connected, keep her present, minimize any discord, and avoid being scolded.

In short, in order to survive, she stopped herself from having certain feelings.

So why would Karen fear that I would think she was bad for having her feelings? I wasn't sitting in judgment of Karen or looking at her with disdain. In fact, I was feeling pretty compassionate toward her, and I'm sure it showed. Yet Karen was still feeling afraid that she'd done something wrong, still worrying that I would think she was bad.

In light of her history, it's easy to understand. This fear is a direct result of her early experiences in which having and showing her feelings *was* a scary prospect. Although the circumstances have changed, on a deep level Karen still anticipates the old consequences. Her system is set up in such a way that now, whenever she starts to feel certain feelings, her brain still sends off a signal that says danger is looming. As a result, Karen often feels anxious and afraid regardless of whether or not such feelings are warranted.

This is exactly what's going on for those of us who are afraid of our feelings. *The fear we have around our emotions is an old fear based in the past, not in the present.* Even though the fear itself is very much experienced in the here and now, our response is really the result of archaic programming. We're still responding as though there were a reason to be afraid, and in most instances there isn't.

Although she could acknowledge her fear in the present moment, Karen had no awareness of the historical roots of her feelings phobia, and that's true for most of us. To begin to turn things around, we benefit from first getting a clear picture of what we're dealing with: the emotional family doctrine under which we have been operating. This is another useful step in becoming aware of our relationship with our feelings.

HOW'S THE WEATHER INSIDE?

Let's take a moment to get a sense of the emotional environment in which you grew up. This was one of the first things that Karen and I did together as well. Consider these questions:

How Did People in Your Family Deal with Feelings?

Were they openly expressive?
Were they more emotionally reserved or private when it came to feelings?
Were certain feelings okay and others not?
Was it okay to be happy but not okay to be angry or sad, or vice versa?
Did people express their anger openly? If not, did they tend to stuff their angry feelings until they reached a certain threshold and then exploded in an angry outburst or flew into a rage?
Did they openly show and express their loving feelings?

Did they hide their grief?

Was it okay for some people to have feelings but not okay for others?

How Did Your Family Respond to Your Feelings?

Were they generally open, attentive, and responsive to your feelings in a positive way?

Did they get uncomfortable or anxious when you expressed your feelings?

Were certain feelings privileged and others not?

Did they fall silent and not respond to your feelings?

Did they divert their attention or walk away?

Did they get irritated, frustrated, or maybe even angry at times when you expressed your feelings? Did they take your feelings personally?

Were they shaming or admonishing in any way?

Did they tell you not to feel your feelings, that they weren't legitimate? Did they get angry at you or punish you for expressing feelings?

Were their responses predictable or erratic?

Overall, did it feel safe to express your feelings?

Your family's attitude toward feelings and the way in which they responded set the tone for the whole social environment. I have found that the *emotional climates* that pervade all families tend to fall into four categories:

1. *Sunny and warm.* The atmosphere in this family is emotionally friendly. People are open and responsive, and it's generally safe to experience and express feelings.
2. *Icy and cold.* In this family, people tend to be emotionally unresponsive and avoidant. The air is bitter and constricted, with no support for emotional exploration.
3. *Stormy.* The weather here is often harsh, with gusts of negativity—criticism, shame, even punishment—in response to feelings. The emotional road conditions are treacherous and unsafe.

4. *Mixed.* Conditions here tend to fluctuate—sometimes sunny and warm, sometimes icy and cold, and sometimes downright stormy—and can often be difficult to predict.

Given Karen's mother's disposition, the emotional climate in which Karen grew up would fall more or less into the "stormy" category. When Karen wasn't hiding behind a smile, the responses she got to her feelings were by and large negative.

Think about your own experience and consider the following questions:

What climate characterized your family? Were people emotionally open and responsive (sunny and warm) or constricted and distant (icy and cold)? Were they negative and critical (stormy) or unpredictably all of the above (mixed)?

Has the feelings climate in your family changed, or is it still the same?

Do you find yourself approaching your feelings in the present in the same way you did when you were growing up?

What is the emotional climate of your own home or family now?

Just as our brain is shaped by the emotional interactions we have with our caregivers, so too is it influenced by the emotional climate of our early social environment. As children, we adapt our behavior to fit in with the prevailing norms of our family culture. With repetition, the resulting patterns of behavior and the respective neural circuitry that gets established in our brain are strengthened over time. Although the social context in which we live changes as we grow up and create a life for ourselves, the road map that gets laid down in our brain lives on inside us and continues to influence our experiences unless we make a concerted effort to challenge it. With an understanding of the emotional context in which you spent your formative years, you will find it easier to identify the beliefs that are constricting your emotional experience and to begin to mount a challenge against them.

The Blame Game?

It's not uncommon to feel conflicted when you begin to take an honest look at the emotional climate in your family of origin. My clients often say things like, "I don't want to blame my parents. They did the best they could. What good is that going to do me now?" I explain that we're not interested in blaming anyone. What we're talking about is looking at, recognizing, and taking stock of your experience, one that inevitably has shaped you and is affecting how you live and love today. It's all about being informed. You can be more in control and make choices that are more authentic—not based on some old, unhealthy "contract" you were too young to understand and that you didn't sign.

When people start to take stock of the effects of their upbringing, they often begin to feel sad, angry, frustrated, or pained. It's natural that you may as well. But these emerging feelings may also be another reason why you're feeling conflicted. The very act of having these emotions, or beginning to acknowledge them, may be going against a family doctrine that has caused you to question and deny your feelings and has kept you emotionally constricted. So feeling conflicted is actually a good sign. You're beginning to challenge the status quo, turn things around, do things differently. You're beginning to break free from unwritten emotional rules (which we discuss next).

In short, honoring whatever feelings you have isn't about blaming your caregivers. It's about acknowledging and respecting your truth. Having these feelings is an important step on the road to resolution and freedom.

UNWRITTEN RULES

Regardless of which emotional climate we grew up in, the messages we got about feelings were likely both explicit and implicit. No matter how they were conveyed, the messages were powerful and perhaps damaging. The more we heard or experienced them, the more they became the unwritten rules that guided our emotional experience. Consider these messages and their implications:

Message	Implication
Being called a "crybaby" when you were tearful	Sadness is bad and brings criticism.
Getting the silent treatment when you were assertive or angry	Anger is bad and leads to abandonment.
Being told "Don't let it go to your head" when you felt good about yourself	Pride or positive feelings about yourself are harmful.
Your parent looking away or leaving when you started to cry	Sadness is bad and leads to abandonment.
Being told "anger is a waste of time"	Anger is useless.
Being called a "wimp" or "sissy" when you were afraid	Fear is bad and leads to criticism.

Do any of these experiences sound familiar? What kind of direct and indirect messages about emotions did you receive? Take some time to consider the messages you got about your feelings and list them on a sheet of paper or in your journal along with related implications.

As you look over your list, ask yourself these questions: *Which messages did I reject, and which ones have I unknowingly taken to heart? Which have become unwritten rules that now control me?* Considering these rules, are they ones by which you want to continue to live your life?

MY HOUSE

Let me tell you a little bit about my family and the messages I received as a child. Although my parents could be demonstrative and warm at times, inwardly they both experienced a fair amount of conflict and anxiety around emotion. My mother, the good Catholic schoolgirl that she was, dutifully learned how to face the world with a smile and a sense of humor, a veneer that barely masked the nervousness and worry that simmered below it. My father, a former captain in the U.S. Marines, hadn't quite left the service behind and took a sort of militaristic approach to child rearing.

I remember one particular Saturday morning; I couldn't have been more than four years old. My father had fixed breakfast for my sister and me as my mother slept in. We were all sitting at the kitchen table: my father reading the paper, my sister compliantly eating her breakfast, and I staring in dismay at my French toast, which my father had just drowned in a pool of maple syrup. I pushed the soggy pieces back and forth as my stomach turned. I didn't want to eat it. *Why didn't he let me put on the syrup myself?* I wondered. The more I fussed, the more irritated my father got. From across the table, I sensed his anger mounting. As I cautiously looked over at him, I saw the scowl on his face and started to cry. The more I cried, the angrier he got, until he finally exploded and yelled, "Don't cry. Act like a man!"

Act like a man? I was only four!

The emotional climate in my house was often mixed, but this certainly was a stormy moment. The message here was clear: fear is bad and shameful. I was also learning lessons that would be repeated and reinforced over time: I must deny my needs; I must not listen to myself or honor my feelings; wanting my own way is wrong and inevitably leads to disapproval, danger, and destruction. No wonder I ended up feeling so conflicted about having my feelings.

UPGRADING THE WIRING

Here's the good news: although we've been molded and shaped by our early experiences, we don't have to remain prisoners of our past. Even though our brain is wired to respond in a certain way, it can still change and grow.[8] That's right—we can actually change the way our brain is wired. Although we can't exactly erase our past programming, we can create new pathways that are able to override what's already there.[9] In other words, we can "upgrade our wiring" so that fear no longer needs to be entangled with the fibers of our feelings.

How do we accomplish this? Just as experience was instrumental in establishing the early wiring of our brain, it continues to some extent to have the power to create new neural circuitry. The key is in having new experiences with our emotions in which we allow ourselves to be more fully present with our feelings and eventually come to experience them free from fear.

As is true of any phobia, the more we avoid what we're afraid of, the less opportunity we have to face and overcome those fears. With feelings phobia, if we keep avoiding our feelings, we'll never know what good can come from being with them; we'll never see that they really aren't something we need to fear. We'll just keep traveling down those old pathways that get us nowhere. For us to change, we need to make a concerted effort to travel in a different direction. We need to find a way to face and diminish our fears and begin to experience our feelings in a new and positive way.

Over time, the more we travel in this new direction, the more we experience and manage our feelings, the more our fear will melt away, and we'll soon be able to be with and share our feelings without feeling anxious. And while we're doing this, we're actually rewiring our brain! We're breaking the old associations between fear and our emotions and laying down new pathways in which having and expressing our feelings are now experienced as something positive. It's as Robert Frost once wrote, "Two roads diverged in a wood, and I . . . I took the one less traveled by, and that has made all the difference."[10]

I'm fully aware that it's hard to try something new, to travel down an unknown path and to feel anxious about doing it. When I finally began to make space for my feelings, I was practically frozen with fear, like the proverbial deer in the headlights. I had no idea of what to expect, and it terrified me. But there *is* a solution that can make facing your fears less scary. The trick is finding a way to begin to reduce your anxiety enough so that you can start to dip your feet in and give being with your feelings a shot. You don't have to jump in all at once. Just a little bit at a time.

AND A ROCK FEELS NO PAIN; AND AN ISLAND NEVER CRIES

Once Karen and I achieved a good understanding of the unwritten emotional rules under which she had been operating, and the ways in which she had been avoiding her feelings, we started the work of addressing and overcoming her feelings phobia. As Karen's anxiety decreased, she began to find the strength to open up to her feelings—long unresolved sadness and anger that had been buried deep inside her—and to do the work of healing. Fairly quickly, Karen's pain began to transform into a renewed sense of her self. She began to feel compassion for the little girl inside her who had suffered so, and her adult voice started to emerge.

After a particularly powerful session, Karen decided to take a risk and talk to her husband about what she was discovering in our work, to share with him some of her feelings. Shortly into her talk, in which she had tried to remain composed, Karen felt sadness and pain welling up inside her. This time, though, instead of fighting them and staying distant as she had done in the past, she gave way to her feelings. She cried openly with her husband, not quite able to fully articulate all that was coming up for her, but clear that something deep had been stirred.

An amazing thing happened. Her husband moved closer, held and comforted her; told her he wanted to be there for her, wanted to understand, and wanted to feel close to her. He told her, "I'd rather have *this* than the island any day."

CHAPTER TAKE-HOME POINTS

- We learn from our early experiences with our caregivers which feelings are acceptable and which aren't, and adjust our emotional repertoire accordingly.
- Our brain is shaped by the exchanges and interactions we have with our caregivers.
- The more positive experiences we have in sharing our feelings with others, the better we get at dealing with those feelings.
- The early emotional lessons we experience are burned into our brain's circuitry and significantly impact how we experience ourselves, others, and the world.
- Our brain is also influenced by the emotional climate of our early social environment, and we adapt our behavior to fit in with the prevailing norms of our family culture.

- By bringing to light the unwritten rules that have been guiding your emotional experience, you'll be in a better position to challenge and break free of them.
- Our brain continues to be malleable and open to growth and change, and through new experiences we can actually change the way our brain is wired.
- Allowing yourself to be present with your feelings in a positive and healthy way rewires your brain so that you'll eventually come to experience them with less fear.

PART 2

Taking Action

CHAPTER 3

STEP ONE
Becoming Aware of Your Feelings

Let's not forget that the little emotions are the great captains of our lives. And we obey them without realizing it.

—VINCENT VAN GOGH

MARK LOOKED DOWN AT THE PIANO KEYS AND STUDIED them for a moment. He could feel his heart beating loudly and the perspiration forming on his forehead. He steadied himself on the piano bench and took a deep breath.

This was it, his audition for the music therapy program at the local university, the only school to which he had applied. It could be a promising moment for him, yet he seemed to feel regretful. Or was it embarrassed? Probably the latter, as he anticipated that he was about to make a fool of himself. But how he truly felt wasn't clear. *Why didn't I practice more?* he asked himself with frustration.

Good question. In the weeks leading up to his audition, he often seemed to find something else to do—running from one thing to the next, whiling away an hour or two chatting on the phone while playing video games. Once in a while he'd sit down at the piano to practice for a bit and then abruptly quit when it got challenging, shrugging it off as ridiculous that he would have to memorize a piece of classical music.

It's not that the audition wasn't on his radar. Somewhere in his peripheral awareness he could sense the clock ticking, and if he let that come into focus, it made him nervous. Or was it excited? He couldn't tell.

Neither could anyone else, for that matter. In fact, to some he appeared not to care. Whenever anyone asked him how it was going he'd either get skittish, change the subject, or say that things were "just fine."

If he'd let himself slow down and sit with his feelings for a moment or two, Mark might actually have been able to get a clearer sense of what he really wanted to do. Ever since he was a child, he always loved making music, especially when his family would get together and sing around the piano. He started taking piano lessons at a young age and was soon leading the family sing-alongs and playing for school concerts and church services. His musical ability and a compassion for others seemed to make music therapy a good match for him. Or did it? He wasn't sure. Well, sometimes he was, but other times he wasn't.

Maybe that's why he barely made it to the audition on time. *What am I doing?* Mark thought to himself. He sat up straight, adjusted himself on the bench, and took another deep breath. He looked over at the evaluator, who seemed to be growing impatient. *I wonder if she can see my hands shaking?* he thought, as he lifted them to the keys and started to play . . .

Whatever, Mark said to himself as he left the room and hurried down the hall. *I guess I didn't want it bad enough.* He grabbed his coat and made a dash for the parking lot. He didn't seem to notice that there were tears in his eyes.

WHEN IGNORANCE IS NOT BLISS

What's going on with Mark? How could he not know what he really wants? Why didn't he prepare for the audition? What's making him feel so conflicted?

Mark's problem is not that he's without feelings. To the contrary, if he'd just scratch the surface a little he'd see that there's a lot going on inside him. And if he were able to spend some time with and make use of his feelings, he probably wouldn't feel so mixed up. There's plenty of energy there that could help motivate him, and more than enough information that could provide some useful guidance.

For instance, maybe he'd discover that he's actually excited about trying to get into this program, but that whenever he gets excited about something he'd like to do, he starts to feel anxious and then distracts himself. If he were able to separate out his excitement and learn how to tolerate his fears, maybe moving forward wouldn't be so scary, maybe he'd feel freed up to follow his dreams, maybe he'd tap into a well of excitement that would energize him to make a go of it and see what he could accomplish.

But that's putting the cart before the horse. The main problem at this point is that Mark isn't even *aware* that he's having feelings. He doesn't recognize or pay attention to the signs. He never stops long enough to notice them and then follow their lead to discover what's happening for him on an emotional level.

At first glance, Mark might seem like an extreme example of someone out of touch with his feelings. But actually, the way he's behaving is pretty common. It's so easy for us to go through life oblivious of the signs that we're actually having feelings. We walk, jog, or race through our day only marginally aware of what's going on inside us. We get wrapped up in our thoughts, questioning ourselves, lost in a haze of worries and contradictions and oblivious to our internal reactions. We get so caught up in the past or future that we don't even notice what's going on in the present moment. And on the occasion when we recognize that we might be feeling something, as soon as we feel the slightest bit of distress, we're back to our avoidant strategies.

The time has come to do something different. If we really want to get somewhere good, somewhere better, we need to open our eyes and wake up to what's going on inside us. We need to put the brakes on, slow down, and tune in to our internal experience. In short, we need to develop what I call *emotional mindfulness.*

EMOTIONAL MINDFULNESS

The concept of mindfulness is not new. It's been around for decades, with roots that go all the way back to the contemplative practices of both eastern and western spiritual traditions. In recent years it has become popular not just in the field of behavioral medicine but among the general public as well.

Our attraction to mindfulness probably has a lot to do with a growing dissatisfaction with our quality of life. The deadening effects of our current culture of multitasking, high-tech distractions, and increased life demands—the inevitable fallout from living mindlessly—are catching up to us. Many of us are eager to find a way to bring some vitality back into our lives. In addition, ample scientific proof demonstrating that mindfulness has the power to improve our physical, mental, and social well-being has further contributed to its popularity.[1]

What exactly is mindfulness? Jon Kabat-Zinn, a leader in bringing mindfulness into the mainstream of modern medicine and founder of the Mindfulness-Based Stress Reduction program at the University of Massachusetts Medical Center, defines mindfulness as "Paying attention in a particular way; on purpose, in the present moment, and non-judgmentally."[2] The nonjudgmental aspect of mindfulness seeks to free us from the intellectual analysis and self-criticism with which we so often react to ourselves, the ongoing commentary and chatter in our head that alienates us from our felt experience. The idea of paying attention on purpose recognizes that it takes effort not to get caught up in our habitual ways of responding but to stay clear and focused. Mindfulness encourages us to let go of our absorption in the past and our dreams for the future and really allow ourselves to fully embrace the present moment. It involves getting curious about one's experience as it's unfolding, not thinking about it, but just noticing and observing it. In essence, mindfulness is open-minded, focused attention on our here-and-now experience. The practice of mindfulness seeks to increase our ability to be more wholly engaged in the present moment—fully awake and aware.

Emotional mindfulness, as the phrase implies, applies the basic principles of mindfulness to our emotional experience. Simply put, it's about purposely paying attention to our physically felt emotional experience as it happens. For instance, noticing when a feeling rises up in you and what this is like. Noticing when and where you feel constricted, where energy stops and where energy flows. Noticing when your face heats up, your chest aches or expands, your breathing changes, your arms tingle, your legs tremble. Noticing how you react to your experience—noticing whatever is there and seeing what happens. The aim of emotional mindfulness is to help us be more consciously aware of our feelings and, ultimately, more fully present with them.

How do you do this? You start by slowing down, going inward, and just noticing. Later in the chapter, we'll be discussing the actual process, as well as the core emotions and the ways they commonly manifest themselves in our body. But for now, the first step is just to accept that the key to awareness of our emotions is rooted in our bodily experience—not in our mind. Emotional mindfulness sounds simple, and in a way it is, but it takes practice. However, it doesn't have to be burdensome or to feel like homework. You don't have to set aside a great deal of time every day to make it happen. It can be done anytime, anyplace. You just need to stop for a moment and check in with yourself.

One of the first hurdles to emotional mindfulness has to do with what I call "making room"—clearing away the clutter so you can see what's going on. When there's too much happening, when two, three, five things are going on at once, it's impossible to notice what's happening inside. We need to slow down for a moment, make some room, and then do one thing and one thing alone: tune in to our body.

You may be wondering why I put so much emphasis on the body. Although emotions originate in the brain, we experience them first in our body. It's why they're called "feelings." They make themselves known through energy, sensations, and bodily reactions, and we *feel* them. At times, our emotions come upon us so rapidly and with such intensity that there's no denying their existence. At other times, however, their presentation can be vague. If you have feelings phobia, emotions can be difficult to detect, as they're often hidden by anxiety. But the discomfort we feel can actually be a useful tool, a signpost that our emotions are not far away. Mindfully tuning in to body sensations increases our conscious awareness of our feelings, opens us up to new information, and brings us closer to our core emotional experience.

IT JUST DOES THAT SOMETIMES

It was five after the hour of his appointment, and I began to wonder where Mark was. Then I heard him coming down the hall. Well, what I heard was his voice on his cell phone as he approached the waiting room, growing louder as he got closer.

"Yeah, yeah, okay, sounds good. Look, I need to get going. I'm at an appointment," and with that he burst through the door and hurried into my office. "I'm sorry I'm late. I hit some traffic on the way over and then I got a phone call as I was pulling into the parking lot. I probably shouldn't have taken it, but it was from my brother. We're getting together after this." He let out a big sigh as he threw his coat and backpack on the couch and sat down across from me.

Mark first came to see me a few weeks prior to this visit, about a year after he had had his audition for the music therapy program. He told me that his life was a "mess" and that he hoped that I could help him figure out what he wanted to do and get some sense of direction. It didn't take long to see that Mark was pretty disconnected from his emotional life. Recognizing that he had a feelings phobia, I was trying to help him become more aware of his feelings.

After settling in, he started to talk about his brother, whom he described as being quite different than him—"a jock, competitive, and conservative."

"How are you feeling about getting together with him?" I asked.

He crossed his legs, and his foot started nervously bouncing up and down. "Um, all right I guess," he responded with a shrug. "I mean, we're just going to have coffee." His body seemed to convey something different as he tensed up and looked away.

"So you're feeling fine about it?" I asked, not convinced.

He looked back at me and said, "Yeah, for the most part."

"Well, you don't look so fine. What's going on with your foot?" I asked, hoping to help Mark become more mindful of his felt experience.

He looked at his foot and noticed it shaking, uncrossed his legs, and put both feet on the floor. "Oh, it just does that sometimes," he said uncomfortably and then looked out the window again. "I've got a lot going on. I guess I'm feeling stressed. I've been thinking that I should really get back to the gym. That always helps. But then I wonder when the hell am I going to fit that in? I mean, I should probably try to go before work, but then . . ."

I could see that Mark was getting caught up in his thoughts and losing sight of some useful information, so I interrupted him and tried to get him to focus back on his body. "Well, maybe it has something to do with being stressed, but your foot started shaking right when I asked you how you were feeling about getting together with your brother. Did you notice that? Perhaps, in this moment, it's telling you something. Why don't you take a minute and try to pay attention to what's there. Give yourself some room to see what you notice going on inside you."

He sat for a moment and seemed to be focusing inward. I wondered what he might touch. After a moment he sighed and said, "I guess I'm not really looking forward to seeing him." As he turned toward me, and I could see that he looked distressed.

LEFT OR RIGHT, WHICH WAY SHOULD I GO?

By beginning to pay attention to his body, by becoming more mindful of his felt experience, Mark is on the road toward greater self-awareness. Clearly he has some feelings toward his brother that are not easy for him to look at and are making him uncomfortable. Who knows what we'll discover, but at least now we're headed in the right direction—toward his feelings, instead of away from them.

Like many of us, one of the traps that Mark falls into is to overthink things. He can all too easily get preoccupied with worries or concerns, trying to examine a dilemma from every possible angle, running it over again and again in his head. It's a pretty common habit. We're so used to focusing on our thoughts instead of spending time with our feelings that it can be quite a challenge to quiet the chatter in our head and shift our attention to our felt experience. The truth is, the more lost we get in our thoughts, the further we are from connecting with our emotions.

Let's talk a little about the brain again. But I need to start off by making a slight disclaimer.

When people talk about the brain, there's a tendency to make generalizations about which side is in charge of what. In reality, it is not so black and white. There is much more overlap. For many different functions, both sides of the brain make important contributions and work together.

Now, having made this qualification, I can also accurately say that the different sides of the brain do indeed have different strengths. For instance, the left hemisphere of the brain—the "verbal" side—is a sort of hub for logical, linguistic, and linear processing. It is less sensitive to our bodily state and reactions and is therefore able to use reason and analysis to make sense of our experience. The right hemisphere is particularly attuned to sensations, sounds, and images—the nonverbal language of emotion—and, as such, is deftly able to read our felt experience.

The upshot of this neurological design is that when we are attempting to be more fully aware of our emotions, the right side of the brain is our friend, and the left side can be a bit of a troublemaker. When we focus on our thoughts—which originate in the left brain—we can get caught in our head thinking about things and lose touch with the somatic sensations, the visual imagery, the bodily reactions (for example, changes in our muscles, stomach, intestines, heart, and lungs) that are a part of our emotional experience. Thinking makes it harder for us to connect with our feelings. It's not that thinking is a bad thing, but when we're trying to be mindful of our emotional experience, it can be a hindrance. If we want to be more aware of our feelings, we need to quiet the left side of the brain and let the right side have some room.

Of course we can't just flip a switch and turn a side of our brain on or off. But we certainly can choose where we put our attention. We can shift our focus away from our thoughts and make some internal space to tune in, observe, and listen to what's going on in our body. In short, our main goal at this point is not to think but just to notice. This approach is at the heart of mindfulness.

Bottom Up Versus Top Down

Another helpful guide to follow to cultivate emotional mindfulness is to work from the "bottom up."[3] Visualize it this way: thinking happens in your head (the top), and feeling happens at the level of your body (the bottom). For most people, our usual mode of operation is to work from the top down, to think about things first and then figure out how we feel. Well, you know where that gets us—stuck in our head and out of touch with our heart. A more emotionally mindful approach is to work from the bottom up, from the level of our felt experience, what we're feeling physically, up to the level of thought. In short: feel first and then think about it.

Try this: zoom in on your felt experience, notice what you're feeling in your body, how it's reacting, and what it wants to do. Scan your body and see what you feel. Notice any sensations in your neck, chest, arms, legs, and elsewhere, and listen to them, listen to what they are trying to convey. Make space for your felt experience and see where it takes you. Later, reflect on your experience; explore what it was like for you, where it came from, and where it brought you. As you consider your experience, let it make sense of itself, let meaning emerge organically.

CHOICES, CHOICES, CHOICES

I never really liked the color I had chosen to paint our living room. I wanted something golden and warm, but what I finally chose, after much deliberation, ended up looking yellow—canary yellow. I thought I'd get used to it, but I never did. It just wasn't me. It's not that I don't like bright colors, but when it comes to the walls in my house, I think it's safe to say that I'm more of an earth-tone kind of guy. So it was only a matter of time before I just couldn't stand living in Disneyland anymore and decided to repaint. I took a trip over to the local paint store to find the perfect color.

This time I'll get it right! I thought as I pulled into the parking lot. But my confidence was short lived. As I marched through the front doors, I came face-to-face with two giant walls of color swatches. Hundreds of them. Each with five, six, seven different shades of a similar color. Now I'm sure some creative type would be thrilled with the plethora of choices, but I was not. It made me start to panic. *How the heck am I going to chose?* I thought to myself as I collapsed into a chair, bewildered.

Then, as luck would have it, I spotted a stack of brochures on the table next to me. I picked up the first one: "Interior Inspirations." I opened it and discovered a small collection of perfectly lovely paint colors, two dozen at most. *Now we're talking,* I thought as a sense of calm washed over me.

Sometimes there is such a thing as too many options.

BACK TO BASICS

When I first ask some of my clients to tell me what they are feeling, they're stumped. It's not that they aren't having feelings— even though they often "feel" that way—they're just not sure what to call them.

One of the problems is that they feel overwhelmed with choices. They think there are a million different options, and, just as I felt in the paint store, they don't know where to start. But that is a trap. There really aren't that many choices. Although it may seem as though there are as many different feelings as there are colors on those two walls of paint swatches, they really are all just variations and blends of a few emotions.

Although some theorists disagree about which emotions should make the list, in general the spectrum of our emotions is actually made up of eight primary feelings and their related shades and combinations. They are

- *Anger:* irritation, annoyance, frustration, exasperation, dislike, resentment, rage
- *Sadness:* disappointment, dismay, loneliness, hurt, despair, sorrow, grief, dejection
- *Happiness:* contentment, satisfaction, amusement, enjoyment, enthusiasm, excitement, pride, delight, joy, elation, euphoria
- *Love:* friendliness, caring, affection, tenderness, compassion, desire, passion

- *Fear:* concern, nervousness, worry, wariness, anxiety, distress, terror, dread, panic, fright
- *Guilt-shame:* embarrassment, regret, remorse, humiliation, mortification
- *Surprise:* amazement, astonishment, awe, wonder, shock
- *Disgust:* contempt, disdain, aversion, distaste, revulsion

Each of these eight basic emotions serves as a sort of short-hand for a range of feelings. As you looked over this list, you may have noticed that the various feelings in each of the groups can be seen as falling along a continuum. For instance, anger might start out as annoyance or irritation, but if we continue to be threatened or thwarted, it can grow to a point where we're feeling enraged. In both cases, at the core we're feeling anger, but rage is a much more intense version of anger than irritation. Similarly, in the case of sadness, if we were to experience a minor loss, such as not winning the lottery, we might feel disappointed (depending on how much the jackpot was!). But a much greater loss, such as the death of a loved one, would cause us to feel grief. Again, in each situation, we're feeling a degree of the same feeling—in one case less, the other more.

You can use these basic emotions to simplify the task of figuring out what you're feeling. While you might think that having a wide range of options to pick from would be desirable, too many choices can actually make the process of discernment more confusing than it needs to be, especially when your feelings are vague. When feelings come on strong, it's not as hard to determine what you're experiencing. But when they are muted, muddled, or hidden, as is often the case when they are entangled with fear, it's hard to tell. It's far easier to identify what's there when the possibilities are few rather than in the hundreds. Besides, the basic emotions actually cover most of the necessary bases and are all you really need for now.

In fact, for the purposes of our discussion, we're more likely to focus on the first six. In general, most people don't have much of a problem with experiencing surprise or disgust. These are not usually feelings that cause a great deal of anxiety. That's not to say that the different strategies you're learning in order to overcome feelings phobia can't be applied to every feeling, because they absolutely can. This process is broadly applicable, and fear can become associated with any feeling, but the following six feelings are the ones that seem to present the most problems for people:

Anger	Sadness	Happiness
Love	Fear	Guilt-shame

Although this may seem like a limited range, I'm confident that you'll see just how much ground you'll be able to cover with these basic feelings.

Aren't Guilt and Shame the Same Thing?

Although guilt and shame belong to the same family, they differ in a fundamental way. In general, shame has more to do with how you feel about yourself than about something you did. Guilt has to do with the latter. We feel ashamed of ourselves, but guilty for doing something we probably shouldn't have done. It's the difference between "I'm a bad person" (shame) and "I did something bad" (guilt). It's for this reason that I've let them stand alone but together as *guilt-shame*. I don't want this distinction to become overlooked or blurred.

You may be wondering why fear is on the list. Isn't fear the very thing we're trying to overcome? Yes, it is—when it's not warranted. But sometimes being fearful is an adaptive response to have. For instance, we should feel afraid when we're in real danger; it prompts us to do what we need to do to get to safety. However, in the case of a feelings phobia, we can also be afraid of feeling fear. We may experience it as weak, wimpy, foolish, or unmanly, so we fight it, clamp down on it, and try to make it go away. This reaction doesn't allow us to learn how to deal with and usc our fcar to its advantage.

What Were They Again?

Having trouble recalling what the basic feelings are? Here's a simple way to remember them. Call them *mad, sad, glad, love, scared,* and *ashamed* or *guilty.* In fact, you can call them whatever you want as long as it's clear what you're dealing with. Remember, the names are just a shorthand for a few different categories of feelings.

LET'S TRY SOMETHING DIFFERENT

Mark told me a little about how, as a child, he looked up to his brother and was always trying to get his attention. His brother, five years older than Mark, was caught up in his own life—playing sports, hanging out with friends, dating—and barely seemed to notice him. As they got older, Mark's brother seemed to make an effort to try to connect with Mark and get together from time to time. But as far as Mark was concerned, their interactions felt awkward and strained.

I could see the sadness in Mark's eyes as he talked; I said to him empathically, "You look so sad."

"Well, I guess. Maybe. I don't know," he said uncomfortably as he shifted in his chair and tried to shrug it off.

"Mark, there are tears in your eyes. That seems to say something. What's happening inside you?" I asked, hoping he would listen to what was coming up for him.

His focus went back up to his thoughts. "I feel like my brother just doesn't get me. No matter what I do, it just doesn't seem good enough for him. Whenever we get together, I always end up feeling bad, and it takes a day or two for me to shake it. I mean, why do I let it bother me? This is just the way he is, and he's not going to change. Why can't I just accept that we're different and move on?"

I could see that this line of questioning wasn't going to get him anywhere. The left side of his brain (thinking) was turned up so high that he could barely hear what was happening on the right side (emotions). I said to him, "My guess is that it's hard to move on when there are unacknowledged feelings inside you that need some attention." This comment gave Mark pause. "So let's try something different, if that's okay with you."

He nodded, and I considered that to be as good a green light as I was going to get.

"Instead of questioning yourself, try putting your thoughts to the side for a moment and just see if you can notice what's going on in your body, what you're experiencing physically."

He sat very still for a moment. His eyes looked downward, and his head dropped slightly forward. Silence for a bit. And then he looked up at me and said, "Well, the back of my throat feels a little funny, kind of sore in a way."

"Okay." *He's on to something,* I thought. "What else do you notice?"

Mark paused for a moment, checking in with himself, and then said, "I don't know; I feel this sort of achy feeling in my chest."

"And if you just focus on that sensation, what happens?" I asked.

"I don't like it. It makes me nervous. I want to move on. But if I'm honest with myself, and you, I guess I'm sadder about this than I realized."

TUNING IN TO YOUR FEELINGS

Mark's beginning to tune in to his body and become more aware of feelings. He's developing emotional mindfulness. As he gets out of his head and makes some room for his heart, he begins to notice the physical signs of sadness (soreness in his throat, achy feeling in his chest) as well as the anxiety he feels when he gets closer to his feelings.

We all experience our feelings a little differently. At the same time, even though my experience of sadness might be different from yours, there are particular sensations and bodily reactions that more frequently accompany certain emotions. For instance, the soreness in the back of Mark's throat that he noticed feeling is fairly common to the experience of sadness. I'm sure it's what inspired the phrases "I've got a lump in my throat" and "I'm all choked up." Whether your emotional experience is unique or similar to that of many others, there is no right or wrong. It just is.

Before we get to the sensations that people commonly experience with their feelings, let's take some time to get a sense of where you are right now in your awareness of your own feelings and their physical manifestations.

Awareness Exercise

Find a quiet place, free from distraction, where you can be free to tune in to what's going on inside you. Get in a comfortable, relaxed position that allows you to be in full contact with the energy in your body. In general, sitting upright with your back straight and supported and your feet against the floor is best.

For each of the different feelings listed here, recall a time in your life that engendered that emotion. If you have difficulty remembering an event or coming up with a memory that evokes some emotion, try using your imagination to create a scenario that would be likely to cause a reaction. You can imagine something happening to you or to someone else, whichever works. I'll also give you a few examples to help lead the way, but don't feel limited to them.

Visualize whatever moment you choose in as much detail as possible. Let the scene play out and let your feelings grow. As you immerse yourself in the experience, pay close attention to what's happening in your body—in your head, face, neck, shoulders, back, chest, arms, stomach, legs, everywhere—and write down the physical sensations that you observe.

If you have a hard time connecting with any feelings, don't worry. That's why you're reading this book! Just observe whatever it is that's there, whatever it is that comes up for you. Keep an open mind and put any judgment aside. If you don't notice anything, that's fine too. This exercise is all about getting an idea of where you are now.

1. *Anger.* Try to remember a time in your life when you felt wronged, when your rights were violated, or when you or someone you love was treated unjustly. Imagine witnessing a violation of some kind or being thwarted in some way from reaching a goal. What do you notice happening in your body? What physical sensations are you aware of?

2. *Sadness.* Remember a situation in which you experienced a loss of some kind. Maybe the death of a loved one, a relationship ending, or someone close to you disappointing you in some way. Or imagine someone you love suffering, having to put down a beloved pet, saying good-bye to a close friend before

you move away. How does your body react? What do you notice physically?

3. *Happiness.* Recall a moment in your life that delighted you, perhaps a time when you won a competition, completed a project with flying colors, or went on a wonderful vacation. Or imagine having a great time with a good friend, doing something caring for someone in need, or simply hearing the sound of a child's laughter. How does your body respond? What do you notice?

4. *Love.* Remember a tender moment that you shared with a loved one, an experience when someone really came through for you, or a time when you felt particularly loving toward someone in your life. Imagine being in the presence of someone you love, looking at him or her with affection, sharing a warm embrace. What kind of physical sensations do you experience?

5. *Fear.* Recall a moment in your life when you were in some kind of danger and there was nothing you could do about it. Or imagine being followed as you're walking alone on a dark and desolate street, being on top of a very high building looking over the edge, or whatever kind of situation would be scary for you. As you stay in that moment, what do you notice happening in your body?

6. *Guilt-Shame.* Think about a time when you broke a promise or said or did something that caused someone pain and sorrow. Imagine doing something you knew would hurt or betray a loved one or committing an act that you believe would be in violation of a strict moral code. Think of the most embarrassing experience you ever had, or picture yourself being humiliated or ridiculed by someone. As you remember or imagine these moments, what physical sensations do you experience?

Okay, now that you're finished, feel free to compare your list with the following descriptions of the common physical manifestations of the six emotions:

Sadness

- Eyelids grow heavy
- Eyes become moist or teary
- The back of your throat feels a little sore
- An achy or heavy sensation in your chest
- Shoulders slouch
- A loss of energy, an all-over sense of heaviness, of slowing down and needing to turn inward

Anger

- Clenched jaw
- Rapid heartbeat
- Increased body heat
- Feeling hot in the face and turning red
- A sense of pressure building up inside accompanied by an impulse to move forward (toward whatever is making you angry), to strike or lash out
- Feeling empowered and strong

Fear

- Cold hands
- Deepened or faster breathing, or holding your breath
- Sweating
- Trembling in the arms or legs
- Tightness in the stomach
- An all-over sense of shakiness
- Increased blood flow to the legs accompanied by an impulse to move back, get away, or run (so you can get out of harm's way)

Happiness

- Smile
- Eyes widen
- An expansive feeling in the chest
- An overall sense of lightness or buoyancy

- Warm feelings inside
- Increased energy
- A sense of enthusiasm and readiness to engage

Love

- An expansive feeling, as though the heart were swelling
- Feeling warm inside, as if you were melting
- Goose bumps or tingly feelings
- Feeling of tenderness toward another
- An inclination to move forward, to embrace and be affectionate
- Feeling calm and content

Guilt-Shame

- Inclination to avert the eyes
- Head may go down
- An impulse to withdraw, pull away, or hide
- An overall sense of heaviness
- Decreased energy
- A sickening feeling inside (with shame, in particular)

Perhaps you have experienced a few of these sensations, maybe more. You may have also noted your unique experience of a feeling not on the list. Great! You're becoming aware of your individual felt experience. You're developing emotional mindfulness.

Remember, emotional mindfulness is a skill and, like any other skill, can be learned and developed. It takes practice.

Here's what you do: at any time you want to, stop and ask yourself, *What am I feeling?* and then tune in to what's happening inside you right in that moment. Not what you think should be happening, not what you wish were happening, but what *is* happening. Consciously direct your attention to your felt experience. When your mind starts to wander or your thoughts start to take over, remind yourself to come back to your body and then do just that. Watch and observe. Each time you repeat this behavior, each time you bring your focus back to your body sensations, you're developing a new habit. You're training your mind to be aware of and pay attention to your emotional experience.

It's important to approach emotional mindfulness from a place of openness, acceptance, and zero judgment. In the world of your emotions, there is no right or wrong. The task is just to be aware and to stay present and focused.

✳

As Mark practiced emotional mindfulness, his awareness of his felt experience grew. Needless to say, there was a lot more feeling inside him than he realized. But in his efforts to open up to his emotions, he also began to discover the many different ways in which he avoided them. And that's where we turn our attention in the next chapter: to our defenses.

CHAPTER TAKE-HOME POINTS

- Unacknowledged feelings negatively affect our experience and behavior.
- With practice, you can become more consciously aware of your emotions.
- Feelings are felt in the body.
- Thinking distances you from your feelings.
- Mindfully tuning in to your body sensations brings you closer to your feelings.
- There are eight basic emotions on which all the others are based.
- How you experience your feelings is neither right nor wrong—it just is.

CHAPTER 4

STEP ONE, CONTINUED
Becoming Aware of Your Defenses

*The walls we build around us to keep sadness out
also keep out the joy.*

—JIM ROHN

JULIE COULD BARELY CONTAIN HERSELF as she left her boss's
office. She hurried down the hall to the privacy of her cubicle,
hoping nobody would notice her as she whizzed by. She wanted
a moment to herself. A moment to sit and take in what just happened, pinch herself and make sure she wasn't dreaming. As she
slid into her desk chair, she could feel her heart racing and but-
terflies fluttering in her stomach. She tried to catch her breath
and slow down.

Breathe, girl, just breathe, she thought to herself.

To her astonishment, Julie's boss had just asked her to move
into a management position. Quite an impressive step up for
someone who had been at the company for less than a year.

I must be doing something right!

For a brief moment Julie felt a glimmer of self-assuredness,
of worthiness, of pride start to grow inside her. It was, in fact, her
dream job. What she had been secretly hoping for. She sat up in

her chair as a smile tugged at the edges of her mouth. The sun shown in through the window and warmed her face.

She picked up the phone and quickly dialed her parents. She just had to share the news with someone.

"Dad?" Her voice trembled with excitement.

"What's the matter, hon? What's wrong?"

"Nothing's wrong, Dad, actually, something good. I called to tell you guys something good."

"What? What is it?"

"My boss just offered me a promotion! I'm going to become the manager of my department."

"Really?"

"Yeah."

"Wow."

Her father fell silent for a moment. It was as if he had disappeared on the other end of the line. Julie began to feel uncomfortable.

"Sounds like a lot of responsibility," her father said. "Are you going to be able to handle that?"

"Uh . . . well . . . sure . . . um . . ."

Julie's heart started to sink. She felt the familiar downward pull on her energy like a giant vacuum cleaner. How many times had this happened in the past? She'd share some good news with her father, only to be met with his doubts, concerns, and worries.

Somewhere inside her, she started to feel angry, but she kept on talking, trying to explain to her father what she would be doing in the new position, why she was right for the job, why this move made sense.

"Well, hon, if you think it's a good thing, I'm happy for you," her father finally offered with what seemed to Julie like feigned enthusiasm.

"Thanks, Dad." More awkward silence, then Julie made some excuse to get off the phone.

Predictable, Julie thought as she hung up. *What did I expect? He always does this,* she told herself. Deep inside, though, her anger started to rise up again. But before it could gain any momentum, she stood up and tried to shake it off. *He means well,* she said to herself. *I mean, I know he wants the best for me. He just doesn't understand.* She vowed to put her father's reaction out of her mind and move on, not to let it get to her.

But as Julie searched inside herself for the excitement she had begun to feel only a few minutes ago, it was nowhere to be found. Where had it gone? In the days that followed, whenever Julie started to feel excited about her new job, she'd also feel anxious. She worried that if she let herself feel too good, something bad would happen and sooner or later she'd screw up. If positive feelings about herself started to rise inside her, she'd begin to feel nervous, uncomfortable, and guilty for letting the promotion go to her head. When she thought about her father's reaction, she'd feel irritated, frustrated, and angry for a second, but then she'd start to second-guess herself, wonder if she really could handle the new position, question whether she was really cut out for it.

Questioning. Debating. Worrying. Hardly what you would expect for someone who just got promoted!

WHAT'S GOING ON?

Julie doesn't realize that she—not her father—has become her worst enemy. She doesn't realize that at this point, she's the cause of her own struggle. While growing up, Julie learned to anticipate her father's negative reactions. Over time, his responses became embedded in her psyche so that now they're a part of her own reaction process. In a way, she now responds to her emotions in the same way her father did. To make matters worse, even though she may be somewhat aware of her feelings, she's clueless about how she interrupts them, pushes them away, and cuts them off. She's oblivious to the fact that she's getting in her own way.

Julie's initial reactions of excitement, pride, and anger are all quite reasonable and appropriate, but because these feelings are making her anxious, she avoids them at all cost. She's afraid to let herself be excited; she's scared that if she does, something bad will happen. She's uncomfortable feeling proud, anxious she'll seem arrogant or conceited. And she's afraid to feel her anger and express it, worried that her father will get upset, that she'll hurt his feelings, and that he won't be able to handle it.

There's so much good that Julie could have if she weren't so encumbered. If she were able to feel proud of herself, she wouldn't be so riddled with doubt. If she could feel excited for more than a few seconds, she'd actually be happy. And if she could allow herself to feel her anger, she'd have the clarity and strength to tell her father how she really feels, and move on.

But what happens instead? Without Julie's realizing what she is doing, when she begins to feel angry, she talks right over it until it's nowhere to be found, or she tries to reason it away, making excuses for her father—*He means well; he just doesn't understand*—when on some level she's still angry. When she starts to get excited, she escapes to the worries she spins in her head, and when a sense of pride begins to grow inside her, she stops herself, afraid that she's acting too high and mighty.

LINES OF DEFENSE

Like so many of us, Julie has unknowingly developed a whole host of strategies to protect herself from the distress she experiences when she starts to have certain feelings. These responses are called *defense mechanisms*.

In some schools of psychological thought, a defense mechanism is defined as an unconscious process employed to avoid unpleasant thoughts, feelings, and desires. In terms of a feelings phobia, any thought, behavior, or reaction used to distance ourselves from our emotions and the anxiety they engender can be considered a defense mechanism or simply a defense. In a way, defenses are coping strategies motivated by the distress we feel when we get close to our feelings and by our desire to avoid that distress. In short, they're a way of coping with fear.

Where Do Defenses Come From?

In Chapter Two we looked at how, as infants, we're extremely sensitive to the ways in which our caregivers respond to our feelings. The fear of a negative reaction becomes associated with certain feelings, and we adjust our emotional range accordingly by omitting or avoiding any anxiety-inducing emotions. Our defensive responses are born during this time; they are our best efforts to manage a difficult situation, maintain a connection with our caregivers, and help us feel safe in an environment that was not accepting of our emotional experiences and expressions. Over time, as we grow older, these defenses become more refined and develop into our "default" responses to feelings. For instance, we may typically respond to our sadness by dismissing it, distracting ourselves, or minimizing the situation that's causing us to feel sad. Similarly, we may respond to our anger by quickly diverting our thoughts or moving on to another topic of conversation as a way of protecting ourselves and others from these feelings.

But notice that I said these defensive strategies were our best efforts when we were *children*. We're not children anymore. What worked for us then may no longer be working for us now as adults. In fact, it's likely that many of our defenses have become outdated. The emotional climate has changed, but we haven't. We're still responding to our feelings as though they're something we need to fear, but they're not. We're still behaving as though we need to protect ourselves and others, but we don't. Our inborn ability to feel is being compromised by obsolete modes of responding, and our emotional growth has hit a dead end.

No wonder we're stuck.

Having said that, we also need to acknowledge that defenses aren't inherently bad. In fact, they can be quite healthy. When it comes to our feelings, we need to have some defenses, or else we'd be emoting all over the place and at inappropriate times. Our defenses can help modulate our feelings and make them more manageable in situations that warrant their not coming out into the open (for example, at work, in a social situation, and with certain authority figures).

When avoidance becomes our standard response to feelings, however, we're in trouble. When we depend too much on our defenses and never learn how to deal directly and consciously with our emotions, we're deprived of the benefits that come from being deeply in touch with ourselves. We end up repeating unhealthy patterns of behavior that leave us disconnected from our true feelings, our authentic self, and the people in our life. Obviously this approach is not a recipe for happiness. In fact, as psychologist and teacher Dorothy Corkville Briggs once said,

"To the extent you hide your feelings, you are alienated from yourself and others, and your loneliness is proportional."[1]

To make matters worse, the longer we rely on our defenses to help us get by, the more deeply ingrained they become. Eventually they just kick in automatically. We respond to our feelings in a reflexive way—as in a knee-jerk reaction—without even knowing it. This lack of awareness is especially problematic because when we don't realize what we're doing, we're robbed of any choice or control. We just keep mindlessly doing the same thing over and over again, wondering why things don't change. Wondering why we can't move forward. We end up at the mercy of our defenses, powerless to do things differently.

Consider Julie's experience. She is not aware that she talks over her anger or that she repeatedly brushes it off when it's still there. Or that when she takes a step toward her anger, she immediately starts to second-guess her abilities and ends up lost in her worries. She doesn't have a clue. If she knew what she was up to, she could then take the steps to do something different, something that could lead her in a healthier direction. For instance, she could begin to deal with the anxiety she feels when she gets angry, learn how to tolerate and make use of her anger, and then respond to her father in a constructive way. Instead, unaware of these patterns, she is trapped in worry, doubt, and fear, all the while wondering why she can't feel excited for very long, why she can't seem to feel truly proud of herself, and why she can't be happy for more than a few seconds before getting anxious.

The Bottom Line

To be able to change our behavior for the better, we need to become aware of all the ways in which we're stopping ourselves from experiencing our feelings. We need to become aware of all the different strategies we've developed to protect ourselves from the fear and anxiety we experience when we get close to our emotions. We need to be able to recognize our defenses.

In order for us to do this, willingness, curiosity, and motivation are essential. We have to be willing to take an honest and open look at ourselves, to get curious about what we've been up to, and to be motivated to do so. If we approach this opportunity for discovery with defensiveness, so to speak, our progress will be thwarted. As Bhante H. Gunaratana points out in his book *Mindfulness in Plain English,* "You can't examine something fully if you are busy rejecting its existence."[2]

Speaking of mindfulness, we can again employ it to help us increase conscious awareness of our behavior. We need to increase our awareness of our emotions and of our responses to them. Practicing emotional mindfulness not only sensitizes us to the presence of our feelings but also brings our avoidant behaviors into the light where we can see them and then, if we want to, do something about them.

In short, being aware of our defenses puts us back in the driver's seat. Awareness restores control, increases our options, and enables us to make a change. Gaining awareness of our defenses is an essential step in the process of freeing ourselves emotionally

---

Give Yourself a Break

When people start to recognize their defenses, when they begin to see all the different ways that they've unknowingly been avoiding their feelings, they sometimes get upset with themselves. If you begin to feel this way, you're not alone. It's not uncommon to feel embarrassed ("How have I not seen this until now? How have I not known what I was doing?"), frustrated ("Why can't I just get a grip and deal with things? Why do I keep on doing this?"), and even ashamed ("What's wrong with me?"). But it's time for a good old reality check. You need to put things into perspective. Remind yourself that your defenses came into play a long time ago, when you were merely a child. You did the best a child could do, and it's not fair to have expected any more of yourself. So give yourself a break! The antidote to any bad feelings that might arise is to practice some compassion for yourself. Imagine yourself as a child, making the best of the emotional climate in which you grew up. Realize that you did your utmost best. Be thankful that you now know otherwise. Now you have a choice. You're an adult with many more options. You can learn a new way of doing things. And you are.

---

and being able to connect more deeply with others. That's important stuff!

So the main objective at this point is to increase awareness of the ways in which we may be keeping ourselves from our true feelings. Let's start by learning a bit about just how defenses operate.

THE SHAPE OF THINGS

Several years ago, Dr. Henry Ezriel, a pioneer in the field of psychoanalysis, developed a way to illustrate the relationship between hidden feelings, anxiety, and defense patterns.[3] This ingenious conceptualization, which has been elaborated by several other theorists, has not only helped clarify our understanding of human behavior but also proven to be invaluable to many therapists in their efforts to help people overcome the conflicts they experience around their feelings. (It's been of great assistance to me, both professionally and personally.) Further, many of my clients have appreciated learning about this simple diagram, as it's helped them better understand their behavior, recognize their defenses, and identify their true feelings. That's why I'm sharing it with you now.

As you can see in Figure 4.1, each corner of the triangle represents one of three different components of our emotional experience. At the bottom corner are our feelings (F). It makes sense that feelings are at the bottom of the triangle; that position shows that they are fundamental, that they come from deep inside us—from the "bottom up." At the right-hand corner is anxiety (A), which is our fear about our feelings; and at the left-hand side corner, our defenses (D). Their location at the top of the triangle indicate how, in real life, anxiety and defenses occur on the surface and cover or mask underlying true feelings.

Figure 4.2 illustrates what happens for us when we get close to a fearful experience of an emotion. Let's walk through the process step-by-step. Something happens in life that prompts an emotional response in us, and a core feeling (F) begins to emerge. As it does, if the emotion is one about which we feel conflicted, a warning goes off inside—"Danger, Will Robinson!"—and we begin to feel anxious (A). As our anxiety increases, it prompts us to run for cover—that is, use our defensive behaviors (D).

FIGURE 4.1: THE COMPONENTS OF OUR EMOTIONAL EXPERIENCE

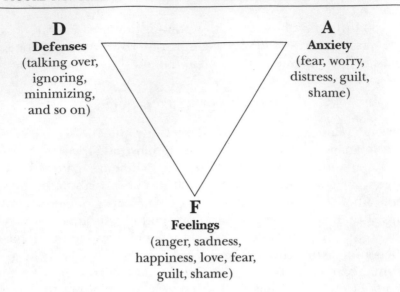

D
Defenses
(talking over,
ignoring,
minimizing,
and so on)

A
Anxiety
(fear, worry,
distress, guilt,
shame)

F
Feelings
(anger, sadness,
happiness, love, fear,
guilt, shame)

FIGURE 4.2: HOW WE RESPOND TO FEARED EMOTIONS

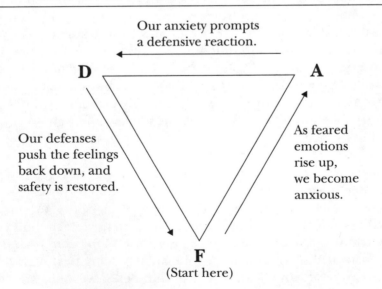

Our anxiety prompts
a defensive reaction.

D   **A**

Our defenses
push the feelings
back down, and
safety is restored.

As feared
emotions
rise up,
we become
anxious.

F
(Start here)

Our defenses rush to the scene and mount a counterattack, pushing our feelings back down enough so that the fear dissipates, and, for a moment, safety is restored—that is, until we start to have another anxiety-inducing feeling and the whole pattern repeats itself. Maybe not with the same defensive strategies, but with the same triangular process.

In Julie's experience (see Figure 4.3), when she shares her good news with her father, instead of celebrating with her, he reacts poorly with doubt and concern. As he questions Julie's ability to handle the new position, she understandably starts to feel angry (F), but on some level, mostly unconsciously, she feels conflicted about her anger and becomes anxious (A). To regulate her anxiety, she keeps talking (D), which effectively pushes her anger down. Later, when she reflects on her father's reaction, her anger (F) threatens to rise up again, which makes her uncomfortable (A), so she responds defensively by making excuses for her father (D), which again pushes her anger back down, out of reach.

Keep in mind that this whole process is usually unconscious (in other words, outside our conscious awareness). Julie doesn't realize that she's avoiding her feelings, and, generally speaking, neither do we. Usually we're unaware of what's going on inside

FIGURE 4.3: JULIE'S RESPONSE TO HER ANGER

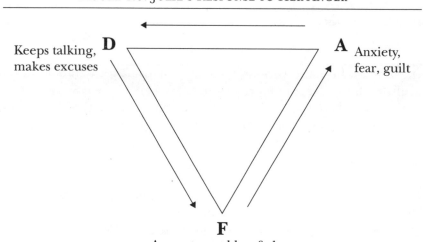

Keeps talking, **D**
makes excuses

A Anxiety,
fear, guilt

F
Anger toward her father

us, that our feelings are causing us discomfort, or that we are responding to them defensively. These things just happen. But as we tune in to our emotional experience, as we practice emotional mindfulness, we become more aware of the discomfort and all the different ways in which we try to avoid it.

Now that you have an idea of how our defenses operate, let's look at some of the ways in which we employ defensive strategies to ward off uncomfortable feelings.

EVERY TIME WE SAY GOOD-BYE

Well, I guess this is it, Brenda thought to herself as they neared the parking lot. She and her friend Emily had come to the end of their weekly walk around the lake, a walk they had taken together hundreds of times. But this time was different. This time would likely be their last walk together for the foreseeable future, as Emily's husband had taken a job oversees, and she was set to join him there in only a few days.

Over the course of their walk, Brenda kept getting flashes of the many moments that she and Emily had shared, of all the times they had been there for each other, the good times and the bad, the ups and the downs. Emily had been her best friend ever since she moved to the city eight years ago, and now she was leaving. It seemed surreal.

In the days leading up to the walk, whenever Brenda would think about getting together with Emily she'd feel anxious, anticipating having to say good-bye to her dear friend and not wanting to face it. She'd shake it off and tell herself that she'd deal with that later when the moment came. But the moment was here, and she didn't feel at all prepared.

They talked and laughed, reminiscing about the fun times they'd shared, but said nothing of their sorrow. At least a dozen times, Brenda felt pangs of sadness in her chest, but each time she pushed them away by changing the subject, distracting herself, or admiring one of the stately houses that lined the lake ("I've always loved that one!"). Then the chatter ran out and left them with an uncomfortable silence pregnant with unexpressed feelings. Suddenly, the reality of good-bye couldn't be staved off any longer.

"I can't believe I'm not going to see you next weekend, that we're not going to just get together like we've always done," Emily said as they stopped right in front of her car.

Brenda felt a lump in her throat and the emotions welling inside her, but she tried to make light of them. "Hey, these days, what with e-mail, we'll always be in touch. We'll probably find more time to connect than ever."

Emily tried to smile; she wanted to believe that was true.

"Well, I better get going. If I don't, I'll start crying, and I won't be able to stop." They hugged, and Brenda felt as though she could melt, but she steeled herself against the torrent inside her and pulled away. She felt as though she just couldn't bear it. Brenda got in her car, smiled and waved at Emily, then looked away. She saw the sadness in Emily's face and couldn't take it in, as it brought her closer to her own feelings. She turned on the radio and drove away. "It will be fine," she thought to herself, as she wiped away her tears.

GETTING TO KNOW YOU

Good-byes are hard. They're especially hard when we're trying to avoid our feelings. When we're not able to be open and share the experience. When we try to play down the moment and minimize the intensity of our loss. What might the pain of good-bye have been like for Brenda if she hadn't had to bear it alone? If she had been able to share her sadness with Emily? I'm willing to bet that they'd have felt even closer, that their shared sadness would have only further honored their love for each other, and that they'd have felt better. Not only because being able to access our core feelings is relieving, even if they're painful, but because Brenda and Emily would then not have been alone in their grief.

Does Brenda's behavior seem familiar to you at all? Perhaps you've experienced it before with a friend or family member. Maybe you've reacted this way yourself. The manner in which Brenda responded to this difficult moment is quite common. Many of us have a hard time allowing ourselves to be present with our feelings during moments of loss. Why? Because we fear that expressing emotional pain will actually make us feel worse. (In fact, the opposite is true.) So, like Brenda, we find ways to avoid the experience. We minimize the moment, we put off our feelings until later—and later never comes, or, when it does come, we can't stop and be present. We simply change the subject and move on when we start to feel uncomfortable.

All these behaviors are defenses.

Learning to spot a defensive reaction in yourself can be very challenging, and for good reason. There are as many different ways of responding defensively to our feelings as there are stars in the sky. In fact, *any* thought, behavior, or reaction can be a defense, so long as it's employed in the service of avoiding your true feelings. Although the possibilities are limitless, there are certain defensive strategies that are more universal than others. Becoming familiar with the more common ones will help you begin to recognize them in yourself, as well as all the other "variations on a theme" that you've undoubtedly developed.

In general, our defenses tend to fall into two categories: interpersonal and intrapersonal.

Between You and Me

Interpersonal defenses are the things we do to keep from showing our feelings to others, and to avoid being emotionally exposed and seen. They include such behavior as

- Averting your eyes or turning away from someone when feelings start to come to the surface
- Smiling or laughing when you're actually feeling something else, such as anger or sadness
- Changing the subject
- Contradicting yourself or minimizing a feeling you just expressed
- Talking rapidly or talking so much that the other person can't get a word in edgewise
- Not talking at all, shutting down, withdrawing, or going silent
- Avoiding specifics and being vague or general about how you feel (for example, "I'm okay" or "I'm fine")
- Being dismissive of your own feelings or the feelings of others ("I seem upset? Nah, I couldn't care less!")

In addition, there are ways in which we physically hold our feelings back and prevent them from being seen. Although there are times when we knowingly brace ourselves against a rising tide of feelings inside us, these physical reactions, like many other defenses, tend to be automatic and unconscious. They include

- Tensing up your whole body
- Physical constriction in certain areas (for example, chest, neck, throat, or jaw)
- Going numb (all over, or in specific areas)

The stories in this and other chapters have illustrated some interpersonal defenses. For instance, Brenda *changes the subject* or *looks away* from Emily when her feelings start to come up. How about Karen in Chapter Two? Remember how she kept *smiling* all the while that she was telling me about the painful problems in her marriage? Mark, whom you met in Chapter Three, was doing a fair amount of *tensing up* and *looking away* when I asked him how he felt about getting together with his brother. And Alex, from Chapter One, *turns away* from his wife when the strains of "Silent Night" trigger his grief. He *grips* the steering wheel, *tenses up his body*, and *pushes his feelings down*.

All these behaviors are defenses. These people are using them to hold their feelings back, avoid sharing them with others, and ultimately circumvent the closeness that comes with being emotionally open and vulnerable. Remember, our defenses originated in an interpersonal context in our early relationships with our caregivers. We carry with us the fear that became associated with our feelings, and we are also afraid of how others may respond to our emotional expression. In this way, we're afraid both of our feelings and of the possibility that whomever we open up to might react in the same way our caregivers did early on—with neglect, disdain, withdrawal, nervousness, hostility, and so on. Real closeness is threatening to us, as it requires emotional honesty and openness.

Do you recognize any of these defensive behaviors as ways in which you hold your feelings back? Take a look back over the list and consider whether any of them seem familiar to you. In a moment you're going to do an awareness exercise to help you get a better idea of how you may respond defensively to your feelings.

Between Me and the Real Me

In contrast to interpersonal defenses, which help us keep our feelings from others, *intrapersonal defenses* are ways in which we keep *ourselves* from experiencing our feelings. They can be a bit more complicated and harder to detect because, unlike interpersonal defenses, which tend to happen in the very moment when feelings are coming to the surface, intrapersonal defenses can be both momentary *and* long lasting. In fact, some of these particular defensive strategies can become chronic ways of responding in which we perpetually keep ourselves away from our feelings.

For instance, remember when I described earlier how I used to keep up a constant pace of running from one thing to the next—from home, to work, to school, to the gym, and home again? That was defensive on my part; all that activity was doing a good job of keeping me from my true feelings, which mainly comprised fear about trusting my judgment and moving forward in my life. And I wasn't just behaving like this from time to time; it had become a way of being for me. I can say this to you now with the benefit of hindsight, but at the time I wasn't aware of how anxious I was under the surface, or that my busyness was actually a massive defense against my fear.

Some of the common signs of feelings phobia that I outlined in Chapter Two are actually intrapersonal defenses. They include

- Overthinking issues, getting "stuck" in your head, not being able to take action (astutely referred to by a client of mine as "analysis paralysis")
- Having to be in control or being overly self-sufficient (otherwise, your strong façade might crack and allow your emotions to come through)
- Avoiding situations that might cause you to have some feelings (for example, not visiting a grieving friend, not applying for a new job because you're afraid of being disappointed, avoiding a family member who has angered or upset you)

- Minimizing the intensity of a situation or experience in order to decrease its emotional impact ("It's really not such a big deal" or, as some of my Midwestern friends are prone to say, "It could be worse.")

- Taking a cold, distanced, intellectual stance when dealing with emotionally evocative situations (for example, attending a funeral of someone close to you, and all you can talk about afterward is the history of the church; a loved one has a serious illness, and all you can focus on is the science of the disease process; talking about yourself in the second person, rather than using "I")

- Being passive-aggressive (that is, expressing your anger in passive ways, such as by being stubborn, showing up late, or "forgetting" to do something)

There are several other ways in which we commonly keep ourselves from experiencing our true feelings, including the following:

- Making excuses, justifying or "rationalizing" away your own (or someone else's) behavior (for example, after not getting a much deserved promotion, reasoning that the company didn't do as well this year as in the past; justifying why you've broken a promise or treated someone unfairly, rather than feeling guilty about what you've done)

- Keeping yourself busy or distracted (watching television, surfing the Internet, cleaning the house, shopping, and so on)

- Blaming or attacking yourself ("I was stupid to have even applied for that job to begin with! I'm such an idiot!")

- Developing or being preoccupied with physical problems or health-related issues even after a diagnosis is ruled out (for example, tension headaches, digestive problems, unfounded worries about possibly having a serious illness)

- Ignoring or denying the existence of an issue, problem, or situation that would cause you to have some feelings (for example, being in a dire financial situation and not paying attention to it, having a chemical dependency problem and denying it)

- Any addictive behavior (alcohol, drugs, food, sex, gambling, shopping, and so on)
- "Acting out" your feelings rather than experiencing or expressing them in a healthy manner (engaging in addictive behaviors, throwing a tantrum, getting into fights, or having unprotected or risky sex)
- Intentionally pushing down or suppressing your feelings

This last defense is a little different from most of the others. When we suppress our feelings, we're actually aware of what we're doing. We make a conscious choice to push our feelings down or avoid them. It can be a helpful defense when we need to rein our feelings in a bit or hold them off until we are in a safe

---

Defense Awareness Exercise

Take some time to increase your awareness of your own defensive ways of responding to your feelings. Look back over the lists of interpersonal and intrapersonal defenses and consider which ones might apply to you. Give yourself some space to really stop and think about whether you might be doing something similar.

Because many of these behaviors are outside our awareness, it might help you to ground your evaluation in reality by recalling emotional times in your life and then thinking about how you reacted. Did you move forward and open up to your feelings, or did you move away? If you moved away, how did you do that? Imagine situations in which you might have some feelings and consider which defenses seem like a likely reaction for you. Which could you easily see yourself doing? Which have you actually done? On a sheet of paper or in your journal, write down the defenses with which you identify. Are there others ways not mentioned in which you characteristically avoid your feelings? Include those on your list as well. Writing down your defenses will help you bring them further into your awareness and reduce the likelihood that they'll remain unconscious as you move forward. On the paper or in your journal, list the five most common ways in which you avoid your feelings.

---

place to experience and express them. But, as is the case with any defensive response, when we overrely on suppression, when we keep pushing our feelings down and never deal with them in a healthy manner, we suffer.

DEFENSES IN ACTION

To get a better sense of how intrapersonal defenses work, let's take a look at a few of the most common ones as they show up in the following stories. The title of each example indicates which defenses are being used as well as the possible feelings being avoided.

Rationalizing and Avoidance as a Defensive Response to Fear and Sadness

Diane hung up the phone and sat down at the kitchen table. Her sister had just called to tell her that their eighty-nine-year-old aunt had just been hospitalized. *This could be it,* she thought to herself. *I really want to see her. She means so much to me.* But then Diane imagined what it would be like to go to the hospital, to see her aunt, who had always been so full of life, sick, lying in bed, connected to all these tubes. She could hear the sound of the heart monitor beeping in her head. Her chest started to ache and then a wave of anxiety came over her. *You know,* Diane reasoned to herself, *she's probably so out of it, she won't even notice if I'm there. What's the sense in going? I'll wait to see what happens.* Her anxiety settled down a bit, and she looked around the room for something to do. She got up from the table and started to empty the dishwasher.

Physical Problems and Preoccupations as a Defensive Response to Anger

Derek looked at the list of projects his boss had just assigned him. It seemed like an unreasonable amount of work to get done in such a brief period of time, but, as was often the case, Derek said nothing when his boss asked him for feedback about the workload. He started to feel irritated as he walked back to his desk and then anxious, stressed. *How am I going to get all of this done?* he wondered. Derek sat down and started to sort through the pile of work in front of him. Suddenly he felt a dull ache in his neck. *Great,* he thought, *just what I need!* By the time he got home from work that night he was in a lot of pain and could think of nothing else. Derek's anger, which could have been useful to him in setting limits with his boss, was nowhere in sight. It had become a "pain in the neck."

Minimizing as a Defensive Response to Pride and Joy

It was the fourth compliment that Michael had received in a span of ten minutes. Everyone was coming up to him, congratulating him on the terrific job he'd done on the fundraiser. One woman went on and on about his special talent at creating such unique and successful events. It was true. Michael had thought the whole thing up himself and had worked for months to create yet another fantastic affair. Somewhere inside him was the beginning of a sense of pride in his work, a sense of joy for a job well done. Yet Michael felt uncomfortable, unsettled, and anxious. This amount of recognition and praise was too much for him to handle. He needed to find a way to put the brakes on. *These people are being way too nice,* he thought to himself. *Anyone could have done this. It doesn't take special talent.* He then looked down at his empty glass and made a beeline to the bar for another glass of wine.

Overthinking as a Defensive Response to (Undetermined) Feelings

Lauren has been struggling to clarify her feelings for Nick, whom she's been dating for over a year. To all her friends and family, they seem like a perfect couple, but Lauren's not so sure. When she tries to get in touch with how she really feels and get some clarity, she ends up stuck in her head, turning her thoughts over and over again. If we could listen in on her process, this is what we might hear. (Notice how she never connects with a feeling, but goes back and forth between her thoughts.)

He's a really good guy, and we have a lot of fun. But something seems to be missing. I don't know what it is. I wonder if I'm really in love with him. I wonder what that even is, *really. I mean, how do you know if you're in love? I could be in love and not even know it, right? Well, I do know I* love *him, but it feels like it should be different. Maybe we just need a break. Maybe I should give myself some space to see how I feel on my own. But he'd probably be so hurt by that. I can just see how upset that would make him. I don't think I could bear doing that to him. Maybe I just expect too much. Maybe if I let myself relax with him more and not worry so much, I'd feel different. Maybe he really is* the guy for me. *But then I think . . .*

And round and round Lauren goes. Where will she land? Nobody knows. And neither does she.

FEELINGS CAN BE DEFENSIVE TOO

Remember when I said earlier that any thought, behavior, or reaction could be used defensively? Well, emotions themselves can also be a defense against feeling. That's right. The very things we defend against can be used as defenses as well. Feelings are defensive when they're used to cover our core emotional experience. For instance, sometimes people respond with anger when they're really feeling an underlying hurt or sadness. Conversely, sometimes people feel hopeless or become tearful—what seems like sadness—when underneath they're actually feeling angry. For any number of reasons, the emotion that comes most readily to the surface is more acceptable or bearable than the feelings that are being hidden, and thus can be used as a defense. In this way, defensive feelings serve to mask what's really happening on a deeper emotional level.

How can we tell if a feeling is defensive? One telltale sign is that it doesn't go away. It keeps repeating, like a broken record, and never comes to a satisfying end. Our anger or guilt doesn't let up. Our sadness or fear doesn't subside. And no matter how much time we spend with the feeling, it brings no lasting relief. Core adaptive feelings aren't like this. They have a forward-moving flow to them and eventually dissipate, sometimes fairly quickly. When we're able to open up to them and feel them through, we experience a sense of relief and find ourselves in a better place.

Defensive feelings don't get us anywhere. Consider Julie's experience. The worry and guilt she felt following her telephone conversation with her father was in part a defense against her core feelings of anger and happiness. She ends up feeling stuck in the defensive feelings and unable to move forward. As hard as Julie tries, she can't shake them. And she won't, until she's able to recognize her defensive response and begin to deal with her underlying feelings.

NOW WHAT?

If you're feeling a little bleary-eyed at the prospect of making sense of your behavior, that's not unusual. Ultimately, it's not so important that you remember the exact categories or names of the defenses we've discussed. I've taken the time to tell you about these common defensive maneuvers to give you a frame of reference to use as you begin to examine your own behavior. What's most important is that you have a good idea of what to be on the lookout for in yourself.

And that's exactly what you need to do now. Your main task at this point is to become watchful. Turn up your sensors and tune in to your reactions. Expand your practice of emotional mindfulness to include noticing how you react to your feelings. Start to notice what you do when you get close to your feelings. Notice what you want to do or feel compelled to do when a feeling starts to emerge. Notice how you respond in situations that could evoke an emotional response. Do you go with the flow? Or do you work against it? Do you listen to yourself with interest, or do you react in a defensive way?

Sometimes you might catch yourself acting in a certain way that could possibly be defensive. You might notice yourself getting antsy, feeling as if you need to move or to distract yourself. You might observe yourself doing or feeling compelled to do any of the defensive maneuvers we talked about in this chapter. Stop and ask yourself what's going on. What just happened that might be causing a reaction in you, might be causing you to feel uncomfortable, anxious, or afraid? If you're not aware of having feelings but suspect something might be going on inside you, check in with yourself about your thoughts, about your behavior. Notice any reactions you might have and get curious. Ask yourself:

What's going on inside? What am I aware of? What do I sense?

What do I notice happening in my body? What sensations am I experiencing?

Am I avoiding something? Am I avoiding a feeling? Do I get the sense that I might be?

Is there something inside I'm afraid to look at or afraid to be with? Is there something inside making me anxious?

If I didn't respond defensively—that is, if I didn't allow myself to retreat—what might I encounter? What might I feel? What might I want to do?

These are investigative questions designed to raise your awareness, to help you tune in to your experience. You may have noticed that some of them are a little vague (What's going on inside me? What do I notice? What do I sense?). That's actually on purpose. Remember what we learned earlier about privileging the right side of your brain when you're trying to connect with your feelings? The open-endedness of some of these questions is to give you a lot of room to notice whatever you might discover, to help you focus in on your felt experience rather than get lost in thinking and trying to understand "why." That could be a trap.

You don't have to be able to answer these questions right now. It's okay to say "I don't know." And it's not so important that you be able to identify what you're feeling; we're going to get to that. What's essential is that you're turning your focus inward instead of away. You're training yourself to stay present instead of finding a way to run. That in itself is a big step.

Turn on your defense radar and leave it on. Let it run in "continuous mode" so that a part of you will be on the lookout, watchful on your behalf. Maybe you'll catch yourself in the moment or maybe after you've responded defensively to your feelings. Either is good as long as you do increase your awareness.

Remember to leave judgment out of it; encourage yourself to stay open minded and allow yourself to see what you do. *There I go again attacking myself. There I go again changing the subject. There I go again making excuses. There I go again getting caught in my thoughts and ignoring my feelings. Was I avoiding something a little while ago? Why was I all tight and constricted at that moment? What caused me to start talking a mile a minute?* And as you notice yourself doing these things, what you now know are defenses, pay attention. Your defenses are cues alerting you to your inner experience. They are valuable opportunities to discover something vital about yourself. As you notice yourself reacting in a way that might be defensive, stop yourself, make some space, go inward and listen. Listen to what's inside you. Stay present and see what you might discover.

As you practice being mindful in this way, you're opening the lens of your awareness to see yourself more completely, and in doing so you're taking control of your own responses. Now you have the opportunity to do things differently. Now you have the opportunity to move in a new and exciting direction toward a more fulfilling, more gratifying life.

CHAPTER TAKE-HOME POINTS

- A defense is any thought, behavior, or reaction used to distance ourselves from our feelings.
- Overreliance on defenses can lead to a variety of problems.
- Defenses operate to protect us from the anxiety we experience when we get close to our true feelings.
- Defenses can be used to keep our emotions from others as well as from ourselves.
- Feelings can also be defensive when they are used to cover up our true emotional experience.
- Practicing emotional mindfulness can increase your ability to recognize your own defensive responses.
- Being aware of your defenses is essential to freeing yourself up emotionally and connecting more deeply with others.

CHAPTER 5

STEP TWO
Taming the Fear

Do the thing we fear, and death of fear is certain.
—RALPH WALDO EMERSON

ON ONE VERY GRAY FALL DAY, I sat in the dimly lit office of my therapist, heart racing, hands tingling, struggling to describe what had been going on for me. She listened closely to me as I laid out my fears in great detail. The more I talked, the more my anxiety increased as I described my doubts about the relationship I was in, my worries about my future, questioning how I felt, what I should do, where I should go. I'm sure I could have gone on and on, but at some point, keenly sensing that the real matter was something else entirely, she leaned forward and stopped me.

"I'm having two reactions to what you're saying," she said. "The first is that I can feel your anxiety. It's very intense, agonizing, torturous really. But it also feels like a wall that, in some way, keeps me from getting to know you. I mean, *really* know you. If you could put that anxiety aside for a moment or two, what's there?"

Her unexpected question took me aback. I shifted in my chair and tried to steady myself. The room, once alive with my nervous talk, fell silent. I could hear the ticking of a clock, getting slower and slower as time seemed to come to a grinding halt. Her intense gaze closed in on me like a camera zooming in for a tight shot.

My eyes darted away from her face to the bookcase next to her as if trying to get away, and then I closed them. I cautiously focused my attention inward, surveying the vista of my inner world to see what might be there besides what I had assumed was there. But it seemed as though there was nothing, just darkness, emptiness—and fear.

I shook my head in answer to her question and then tried again. Shoring up all the courage I could muster, I planted my feet firmly on the floor, directed my attention inward, and listened hard for what might be hiding beneath my anxiety.

DAY OF RECKONING

And so I started, in that quiet but pivotal moment, the work of taming my fear and making room to see what was really inside me emotionally. I didn't know it at the time, but I was about to embark on an experience that would change the course of my life. It was fall 1994, a few months after graduating from my doctoral program, and it seems like a lifetime ago. I was a different person. In fact, as I look back, it's hard even to recognize myself, hard to remember ever feeling that anxious. But I did.

From a very young age, I had learned to doubt my true feelings and to fear the consequences of trusting my feelings and revealing my true self. Although I had managed to move forward and accomplish a great deal, internally I was struggling. On a deep level, I still expected that something bad would happen if I really opened up and completely embraced the fullness of my emotional experience. The old wiring of my brain kept giving off warning signals, effectively reining me in and keeping my truest self from fully emerging.

Without my knowing it, I had developed a million different ways to avoid my true feelings and the fear that they engendered. For quite a while my defenses—staying busy, distracting myself, questioning and rationalizing away my feelings, dismissing or denying them—had worked to keep my anxiety at bay. But something inside me wouldn't let up. The voice of my deepest self was aching to be heard and kept searching for a chink in my defensive armor.

It found a way out on graduation day. In the subsequent months, without the business of my academic pursuits to distract me, the surface had continued to crack. The feelings I had been running from were finally breaking through.

I realized that the time had come to stop running, to slow down, quiet the chatter in my head, and make space for what was going on inside me. If I was going to have the life I really wanted, I had to start to try to be aware of my feelings. Fortunately, I found my way to a wonderful therapist, who was able to help me. It wasn't easy at first, because I had become quite the master of avoidance. In fact, the more I paid attention to what was going on inside me, the more I discovered all the clever little diversionary tactics I had developed over the years. I had had no idea just how skilled I had become at avoiding my feelings.

But I needed to become skilled at something very different. I needed to learn how to loosen the grip that anxiety had over my emotional experience. I needed to learn how to tame my fear.

And now I'm going to teach you what I learned.

BEYOND YOUR DEFENSES

As we become aware of our own defenses, and work to stay present with our feelings, it's inevitable that we'll begin to encounter uncomfortable feelings like anxiety and fear. Maybe this has happened for you already. Perhaps you've become aware of having a sense of unease, or maybe you've experienced something more like dread. Maybe you've become aware of tension in your body, constriction in your chest, rapid heartbeat, or feelings of restlessness. These are all manifestations of fear, the very thing that caused your defenses to develop in the first place.

As we stop doing a defensive dance with our feelings, we get more in touch with the fear we were trying to avoid. Although distress of this kind is not pleasant, it's actually a helpful sign that we're getting closer to our emotions. In a way, it's telling us that we're right on track, that we're beginning to approach our feelings and learn how to deal with them. That we're on our way to a better, richer life.

But first, at this crucial point in the growth process, we need to find a way to decrease our anxiety. If we don't, we may continue to avoid the fullness of our emotional experience and, in doing so, compromise our happiness. That's why it's essential to develop more effective strategies to deal with our distress that put us solidly back in control.

Let's start by taking a closer look at what exactly is happening when we become anxious and afraid.

BACK TO THE BRAIN

In Chapter Two we looked at how our early emotion-based experiences become part of our neural circuitry and, as such, significantly impact how we experience ourselves, others, and the world. When our feelings are met with the threat of abandonment or censure, they become associated with a sense of danger and become part of our nervous system's emotional history "inventory" of what to avoid at all costs.

The amygdala, an almond-shaped cluster of neural circuitry deep inside our brain, is the storehouse for these and other significant emotional memories. It's also the area of the brain that gauges the emotional significance of events, letting us know whether a situation is good or bad, happy or sad, safe or dangerous. The amygdala is relevant to our current discussion because it's the place in the brain where fear originates, *and* it has the powerful ability to overwhelm rational thought, overlook reality, and overtake emotional experience.

The groundbreaking research of the neuroscientist Joseph LeDoux has helped explain how the amygdala is able to "hijack" the rest of the brain.[1] Using cutting-edge technology, he and his colleagues at NYU have shown how, as a function of the way our brain is wired, the amygdala can bypass the neocortex, the "thinking" part of our brain, and alert the body to danger. The amygdala reacts very quickly, sending out signals to the rest of the brain and priming the body for a fight-or-flight response, even before we've had a chance to thoughtfully assess a situation. Our heart gets pumping, our awareness heightens, and our muscles prepare for action, all while the rational part of the brain is still figuring out what to make of things. Eventually our more fully informed neocortex weighs in, but because of its more complex neural circuitry, this takes longer to happen.

This quick-fire response potential of the amygdala, whereby emotion can overcome rational thought, has had survival value. We wouldn't have lasted very long in prehistoric times if we had to stop and think about a dangerous situation before finding a way to safety. The amygdala continues to alert us to danger and mobilize us to respond accordingly.

The problem is, however, that the amygdala's response is often based on outdated lessons from the past, lessons that are stored in its neural library. Its method of appraisal relies on a process of "pattern matching" in which the amygdala first scans our current experience and then runs a search through the inventory of our emotional history to assess whether there's any recorded cause for alarm. If it finds a match in past experiences, even if the match is very remote, it urges us to respond as we did to the original experience.

In short, on the basis of previous experience, the brain predicts whether something bad is about to take place, and our body responds in kind. This process helps explain why we sometimes react to a situation with fear even though there's no reason for us to be afraid. For example, a friend of mine was in a near-fatal car accident when she was in her early twenties. She was closely following a car in front of her when it abruptly stopped to make a turn. Not wanting to ram into this car packed with children, my friend reflexively turned her steering wheel to the right and drove into a telephone pole. Fortunately, she lived to tell this story. But twenty-five years later, whenever she's driving and gets too close to the car ahead of her, she becomes anxious. The same kind of thing happens with our feelings. Because of early negative emotional experiences, our amygdala keeps panicking when we get close to our feelings even though there's nothing to fear.

But this situation doesn't have to be permanent. We can "reprogram" the amygdala to have a friendlier response toward our feelings. Ultimately, we can create a different response pattern. Through repeated constructive experiences with our feelings, we can develop a more positive relationship with them that can become familiar and expected. In doing so, we establish a new frame of reference for our amygdala, in which emotions are no longer perceived as threatening but as something good.

It's like what Dale Carnegie once said: "Do the thing you fear to do and keep on doing it . . . that is the quickest and surest way ever yet discovered to conquer fear."[2]

You might be thinking, *Easier said than done*. I fully understand. It's *not* so easy for us just to drop fear and fully embrace our feelings, especially after so many years of avoidance. This is one of the major costs of our defensive maneuvers. They've deprived us of having productive experiences with our feelings that can extinguish the fear response.

The good news is that we don't have to brace ourselves and soldier forward. That wouldn't really help us find out how to be present with our feelings. Instead, we can learn to reduce our discomfort to a much more manageable level so that the process of opening up to emotional experience is not overwhelming. We can gradually move toward a fuller experience of feelings one step at a time until we're finally able to experience them anew.

Opening up to emotional experience is a process; it can't happen overnight, but with practice and awareness, we can learn to tame our fears, calm our body, and connect with our true feelings. The rest of this chapter is devoted to teaching you several tools that you can use to calm your nervous system as you approach your feelings. They are

1. Identifying and labeling your emotions
2. Mindfully tracking your experience
3. Deep breathing
4. Positive visualization

With practice, these strategies will help you feel less anxious and more able to stay present with and make room for your emotions.

PAUSE FOR STATION IDENTIFICATION

Frank hangs up the phone after a terse conversation with his soon-to-be ex-wife. He feels stunned, confused, and not sure what to do. She just told him that she listed their house that weekend with a real estate agent—the house in which they had lived together for ten years—and that it would be going on the market in a week. They had touched on the subject only briefly a couple days ago, but had hardly arrived at a decision, at least as far as Frank was concerned.

I never said I was ready to sell the house, Frank thinks to himself as he walks into the next room. Somewhere deep inside him, outside his conscious awareness, he starts to feel angry. A part of him wants to rise up and say, "How dare you go ahead and do that!" But that part doesn't surface because his anxiety and worry have already monopolized his attention. Distraught, he paces the house for hours, running the phone conversation over and over in his head. He tries to sleep, but he can't, his thoughts bouncing back and forth, his emotions churning inside him. Frank tosses and turns most of the night and arrives at work bleary-eyed and drained, wondering how he'll get through the day.

Frank's evening would have gone a lot differently had he been able to acknowledge and identify what he was feeling. If at any point after he'd gotten off the phone he had paused to tune in to his emotional experience, recognized his anger, and labeled it as such, he would have been much better off. Simply naming our feelings for what they are is actually a powerful anxiety-regulating tool.

If that sounds too good to be true, picture a young child in a classroom at his desk, wriggling in his seat and waving his hand in the air, anxiously trying to get the teacher's attention. He's full of energy and in constant motion. He can't calm down until she calls on him. "Timmy, do you have something to say?" she finally asks. Suddenly he feels seen, acknowledged. If the teacher does a good job of listening to him, he'll also feel affirmed and gratified as he settles back into his chair.

Feelings are similar to that child. They need to be noticed, they need to be acknowledged, and they need to be identified. Once we tune in to them, once we recognize them and label them for what they are, they often stop vying for our attention; the agitation they generate decreases, and we feel calmer. Had Frank been able to acknowledge and accept his anger, he would probably have experienced a shift, possibly a sense of relief, and then he might have been able to view his options from a different angle.

On a physiological level, simply naming our feelings actually calms the amygdala. Recent research by UCLA psychologist

Matthew Lieberman and his colleagues confirms that attaching a label to a feeling dampens the fear response and thus decreases emotional distress.[3] Acknowledging and naming our feelings— whether they are of anger, sadness, anxiety or fear, happiness, love, guilt or shame, or even just a vague sense of an emotion— enable us to regulate our own nervous system and put us back in control.

WHAT'S IN A NAME?

Remember the basic emotions we looked at in Chapter Three?

Anger	Sadness	Happiness
Love	Fear	Guilt-shame

Having an awareness of these six primary emotions makes it easier to identify what we're feeling. If we're not sure what's coming up emotionally, we can just run down the list.

Sometimes simply paying attention to our felt experience brings our emotions easily into focus so that we can name them, but sometimes what we're feeling is not so clear. When our emotional experience is not readily apparent, carefully considering each of the basic emotions can be quite helpful.

There are times when we may experience more than one feeling. They come to us all at once, in a jumble, and need to be untangled. For instance, one of my clients recognized that he had a confusing mix of feelings following an argument with his partner. As we explored his feelings, he was able to identify feeling angry, sad, loving, and anxious. His anger, sadness, and love were valid responses in light of this disruption in his relationship, but his anxiety had more to do with his discomfort around feelings in general. Being able to identify and name each of these emotions helped him sort out his experience, as well as decrease the anxiety he was feeling.

One of the great things about the process of naming feelings is that when we're able to stay open to our emotional experience, we get instant feedback. It's as if we were taking some kind of exam or survey online, and, after we type in our answer and hit the Enter key, "That's correct!" or "Wrong!" flashes on the screen. The same is true for labeling feelings. If the label doesn't fit, we can tell that we haven't hit the mark because our emotional energy doesn't change. But when it does fit, we can feel it—like a puzzle piece easily snapping into place. We experience a shift in the energy in our body, a sense of relief comes over us, and our anxiety settles down a bit. Of course, all this depends on our ability to be in touch with our feelings.

Let's take a look at what Frank's process might have been like if, following the conversation with his wife, he had tried to identify and name what he was feeling.

Frank hangs up the phone, stunned. He stands still for a moment as the news from his wife settles on him; he then suddenly starts pacing around the house. A few minutes go by before Frank becomes aware of what he's doing. He realizes that he hasn't stopped moving since he got off the phone, and thinks to himself, *I'm getting pretty worked up. What's coming up for me?* He sits down on the couch and focuses inward. Franks notices that his heart is beating quickly and that he's feeling agitated. *Am I anxious?* he wonders, and then tries to calm himself. *Yeah, well that's a part of it,* he acknowledges. But Frank has the sense that there's

---

Naming Tool

When you're feeling anxious or uncomfortable, take the following steps:

1. Notice that you may be having a feeling.
2. Focus your attention inward on your bodily felt experience and stay present.
3. Try to identify and name what you are feeling (angry, sad, happy, loving, fearful, guilty or shameful). If the feeling is not clear, take some time to sit with it; tune in to it and the sensations that surround it.
4. See if the label fits, if the name and sensation "click" into place.
5. When you're able to accurately label your feeling, you'll notice a shift in the energy in your body. Take a moment to sit with this new awareness.

---

something more going on for him. He focuses inward again and notices that he feels the urge to lash out. *I'm angry,* he says to himself, and as he does, the energy in his body shifts. He feels clearer. *Of course I'm angry,* he thinks. *She has no right to put the house on the market without consulting with me!* Frank sits for a moment and allows himself to connect with the energy of his feelings.

You can use the Naming Tool on the previous page to help you identify and label what you are feeling.

KEEP IT SIMPLE

Naming feelings shouldn't be a complicated endeavor. You don't need a lot of words; in fact, just a few can go a long way. For example, *I feel sad, I'm angry,* and *I feel happy* are short phrases that carry a lot of information. These statements all clearly express an emotional experience and leave no doubt about what's going on for you. More elaborate explanations or justifications often lead to talking or thinking *about* your feelings rather than just naming them. For instance, you may say things like, "I feel that my life is a mess." Although this is a compelling statement, it says nothing about how you feel. It can't. It's a *thought,* not a *feeling.* Instead you might say, "I'm feeling angry (or frustrated or sad) that my life is such a mess."

People often confuse thoughts with feelings. We think that we're describing our emotional experience when we're really talking about what we think. This is a surefire way of staying stuck in our head and disconnected from our true feelings. It also does little to diminish the energy that feelings engender when they're trying to get our attention. They keep buzzing about under the surface, and we continue to feel anxious.

When we try to identify what we're feeling and we follow the word "feel" with such words as "that" or "like" (as in, *I feel like . . .* or *I feel that . . .*), we end up expressing an opinion, judgment, or thought, rather than what we're feeling. For instance, if you were to say, "I feel that this situation is so unfair," or "I feel like I did my best," you're not really saying anything about what you feel; you're expressing a thought. How do you *feel* that the situation is so unfair? Angry? Sad? Guilty? How do you *feel* that you did a good job? Happy? Excited? Relieved? These simple adjectives describe a bodily felt experience and, in doing so, describe what you're feeling.

As you try to identify and describe what you're feeling, pay attention to the words you use. If you limit yourself to two or three words (for example, *I'm afraid, I feel ashamed, I feel excited*) and stick to the basic emotions and their family members, you'll avoid falling into the trap of describing your thoughts. You may also become aware of a tendency to focus on what you're thinking instead of staying with your emotional experience. Like many of my clients, you'll begin to catch yourself when you mistake your thoughts for your feelings, enabling you to refocus and get back on track.

Thoughts Versus Feelings

Here's a little test. If, when you're trying to identify how you feel, you can substitute the word "think" for the word "feel" and it still makes sense, you're expressing an opinion or thought, not a feeling. For example, saying "I *feel* that I'm being treated unfairly" also works as "I *think* that I'm being treated unfairly." Both statements are expressing a perspective or an opinion. Neither says anything about how you feel about being treated unfairly. So keep it simple, avoid "that" and "like," and you're more likely to hit the nail on the head.

WHEN THINGS AREN'T CLEAR

Sometimes feelings are not so clear. Sometimes they come to us as a vague sense that there is something going on under the surface. For instance, in addition to feeling angry about his wife's putting their house on the market, Frank probably has sad feelings of loss and grief that may not be readily apparent to him. He might notice that there's something emotional percolating inside, but is unable to identify these other feelings. At moments such a these, just acknowledging the presence of emotion—*I'm feeling something*—can decrease anxiety. You can imagine leaving the doorway of discovery propped open, to send the message to your system that you're open to finding out. There's something about letting yourself know that you want to learn what you're feeling that gives your emotions permission to eventually emerge and make their identity known.

In contrast, when we close the door on our potential awareness by giving up, by saying we don't care, or by dismissing the possibility that we might be feeling something, we thwart what could be a naturally unfolding process. Our emotional energy backs up inside us, and we end up feeling distressed—much like that child in class, needing to be acknowledged.

You can use the Staying Open Tool to help yourself remain open and to encourage a vague feeling to clarify itself.

Staying Open Tool

When you're not able to identify what you're feeling, take the following steps:
1. Acknowledge to yourself that you are feeling something.
2. Let yourself know that you're open to finding out. Say to yourself:
   I'd like to know what I'm feeling.
   I'm open to finding out.
   I'll wait and see what comes.
3. Leave your emotional radar on and stay receptive to an answer when it arrives.

MINDFUL TRACKING

Frank came to see me when the stress of his divorce had become unmanageable. Embarrassed, he shared with me that one of the problems he encountered in his marriage was that it was hard for him to open up emotionally. Frank frequently second-guessed himself and spent a lot of time in his head rationalizing away his feelings; he was often at a loss to identify what was going on inside him. He painfully disclosed that his wife had described him as "emotionally distant" and had given up on trying to connect with him. In reality, Frank was not without feelings. He was just very anxious about having them and didn't know how to be with his emotions or make good use of them.

Through our work together, Frank became more aware of his feelings and recognized the ways in which he avoided or interrupted his emotional experience. While identifying and naming his feelings and focusing on his breathing helped Frank better manage his anxiety, he also benefited from paying attention to his physical experience of anxiety. At first, this strategy seemed counterintuitive to Frank. *How could paying attention to my anxiety make me feel better?* he wondered in disbelief. *Won't that just make it worse?* I explained to Frank that if anxiety is acknowledged, it will decrease in intensity. Mindfully *describing* and *tracking* the physical manifestations of anxiety help us regulate our emotional experience and get a little distance from it. Frank's skepticism began to melt away when he gave it a try and saw that simply describing his physical experience of anxiety markedly decreased his distress.

When we're feeling afraid, we're at risk for getting lost in our fear and feeling overwhelmed and helpless to do anything about it. Taking an observant stance and describing what's going on for us help us separate a bit from our discomfort and regain control over our experience.

Imagine standing on a dark stage with a bright spotlight above you illuminating a circle of light on the floor. If you stand inside the circle, you are saturated with the light, and it's difficult to see. If instead you step outside the sphere of light, you can get a better look at it. You're able to observe and describe it while not being blinded by it. This is what happens when we're able to reflect on our emotional experience. We're able to step to the side, see more accurately what's happening in the moment, and avoid being overwhelmed by it.

When we're trying to open up to and explore our feelings, we can use the language of observation to help decrease our anxiety. For instance, if we were able to listen in on Frank's thoughts, here's how he might use mindful tracking both to observe and to modulate his distress. He might say to himself, *So, I'm just noticing that I'm starting to feel a little anxious. Maybe more than a little. My heart is also beating quickly. I can feel it in my chest. Now I notice that my breathing is kind of shallow, kind of tight. It feels like something is sitting on my chest. Something heavy. Just saying that, though, I notice it relaxes a bit and doesn't feel as intense. It opens up some. Now I notice . . .*

As you can see, Frank is just verbalizing what's going on inside him. He's not judging it, trying to figure it out, or make it stop. By simply observing and putting his experience into words, he's effectively reducing his anxiety and getting some control of his experience. You can use the Mindful Tracking Tool to help you manage your anxiety when you're trying to explore your feelings.

Mindful Tracking Tool

When you notice that you're feeling anxious or fearful, take the following steps:

1. Focus in on your bodily felt experience (for example, clenched jaw, constriction in your chest, tingling in your hands, racing heart, difficulty breathing).
2. Without question or judgment, notice and describe to yourself what you're experiencing physically. You can use the phrase "Now I notice . . ." to lead you along in your process.
3. Notice how the sensation shifts—or not—when you attend to it.
4. Continue to track and describe your experience until your anxiety or fear settles down a bit. If you continue to feel anxious, you might want to try some of the other exercises in this chapter.
5. When you are feeling sufficiently relieved, take a moment to sit with and appreciate this shift.

TAKE A BREATHER

Vicki came to see me during a difficult time in her life. She was struggling in her relationship with her eldest daughter, who was about to leave for college. Up until this point, they had been very close, but lately, as her daughter's departure for school neared, she seemed to be pushing Vicki away. Vicki was filled with a mixture of emotions. She felt sad about the distance she was experiencing with her daughter and the inevitable loss of both physical and emotional closeness between them. She also felt angry with her daughter for being unreasonable at times, as well as conflicted about having any of these feelings. She just wanted to enjoy what little time she had left with her daughter.

It was difficult for Vicki to allow herself to fully acknowledge and be with her emotional experience. Whenever I asked Vicki about what she was feeling, she would get anxious and tense. In fact, I noticed that when she got closer to her feelings, she seemed to hold her breath momentarily. It was as though stopping herself from breathing was an automatic shutoff valve for her emotions—if she'd just hold her breath long enough, maybe they'd go away. When I called this response to Vicki's attention, she was surprised, but admitted that it was true. I explained to her that this response was a physical manifestation of fear—her body was tensing up as her feelings neared the surface—and that she could regulate this reaction by paying attention to deepening and slowing her breathing. Vicki's experience quickly shifted when she was able to keep breathing, and she eventually felt less afraid and more willing to open up to and spend some time with her feelings.

Vicki's tendency to hold her breath and restrict her breathing is not uncommon. I see this all the time. As people begin to feel anxious about their feelings, their breathing changes; they may hold their breath or breathe more rapidly, high in their chest. It's a natural response to something we fear. What's remarkable though is how much and how often we're not even aware when this is happening. It's an automatic response to our emotions.

Most of us don't pay a lot of attention to our breathing, but we should. Our breathing patterns not only reflect but also *contribute* to our emotional state. For instance, as I've become more aware of my breathing, I've noticed how it changes when I'm feeling anxious or stressed. My breathing becomes shallow, and my chest feels tight. If I don't pay attention to this anxious response, it can feed on itself—my breathing gets more constricted as my anxiety rises, and my anxiety becomes more acute as my breathing gets shallower and my chest tightens up. I have found that a simple way to help calm myself when this is happening is to concentrate on breathing lower, from my abdomen. When I do this, my anxiety decreases considerably, and in a relatively short period of time I'm feeling more relaxed.

How is it that breathing more deeply can so alter our experience? The answer has to do with our autonomic nervous system, which helps us adapt to changes in our environment. When we're feeling threatened in some way, the sympathetic branch of our nervous system goes into action—heart rate and blood pressure increase, muscles tense up, and breathing becomes rapid and shallow—readying us to fight or flee. The parasympathetic branch of our nervous system is what calms this response and causes us to relax. Breathing deeply is the fastest way to stimulate the parasympathetic nervous system and reverse the activation of a fear response. In fact, research has shown that the slow exhalations produced by mindfully attending to our breathing actually reduce activity in the amygdala—our fear center.[4] Moreover, deep abdominal breathing promotes an overall sense of calm and ease, can bring us to a place of deep relaxation, and, as psychiatrist Henry Emmons points out in *The Chemistry of Joy*, it has "marvelous effects" on our brain chemistry.[5] It's just plain good for us!

You can use the Breathing Tool when you are getting in touch with your feelings and start to feel anxious or afraid. When you notice yourself tensing up, concentrate on deepening your breathing and letting yourself relax. It's also a good idea to practice abdominal breathing for a few minutes every day, as this reinforces and strengthens your ability to calm yourself more readily.

Breathing Tool

When you're feeling anxious or afraid, take the following steps:

1. Focus in on the tension in your body.
2. Place your hand on your belly, right below your rib cage.
3. Breathe in slowly through your nose and let the breath go all the way down into your abdomen. You will notice your hand rise if you are doing this correctly.
4. Pause for a moment after fully breathing in and then, as you slowly exhale, allow your body to let go.
5. Repeat this process several times, focusing on your breath and allowing it to freely go deeper and deeper. Encourage yourself to relax fully and stay focused on your bodily and emotional experience.

ACCENTUATE THE POSITIVE

As I write this section, I'm sitting on the couch in our sunroom on a cold winter day. On the floor next to me sit our two little dogs—Maisy, a Cairn terrier, and Rusty, a Norwich terrier—arguably the most adorable dogs in the world. (I know. I'm a proud parent.) Just looking at them for a moment warms my heart and fills me with affection toward them both. They're quite a pair and bring a lot of love and laughter into our home and into our lives. At my work office, I have a picture of them on my desk. Sometimes when I'm busily working, I'll glance over at their photo, and that same warm feeling will come over me. If I'm feeling tense or stressed, one look at their big brown eyes instantly takes the edge off, like a soothing balm to my soul.

Mental images and the feelings they engender affect our emotional state. Whether it's picturing a beloved pet, a happy time spent with loved ones, or imagining being on a dream vacation, positive images can evoke an emotional experience that fills us with pleasure and delight. They can also ease anxiety. Research by Kerstin Uvnas-Moberg, a Swedish neuroendocrinologist, showed that calling to mind positive mental images of a loved one releases oxytocin into our system.[6] Oxytocin is a neurochemical that decreases the release of stress hormones and reduces activation of the amygdala.[7] Therefore, turning our attention to positive mental images is calming and thus can be a powerful tool for taking the edge off of fear.

In recent years, the field of positive psychology has begun to examine the influence that positive emotions (happiness, love, contentment, gratitude, and so on) have on our overall well-being. This area of study is a welcome advance in the field of psychology; for far too long, our attention had been mainly focused on understanding and dealing with what makes us feel bad. It seems obvious that we should also understand what helps us feel good. We are beginning to appreciate just how fundamental positive emotion is to our psychological and physical health. For instance, in addition to making us feel better, positive emotions enhance resilience, intuition, and creativity, and actually increase our longevity.[8]

Positive emotions can also help us cope better with difficult situations. In particular, they can be an effective antidote to anxiety and fear. Research by psychologist Barbara Frederickson at the University of Michigan shows that experiencing positive emotions—such as mild joy and contentment—can decrease the physiological effects of negative emotion.[9] For example, the rapid heartbeat we experience when we're afraid can be slowed down by picturing something that evokes positive feelings. This process is known as visualization because we are visualizing someone or something that evokes a positive feeling.

Visualization can help us manage the anxiety we encounter as we open up to our feelings. Calling to mind positive images and connecting with the pleasurable feelings they generate can effectively counteract fear, but we don't have to wait until we're feeling anxious to try to bring up positive images.

Visualization will be easier to do when we have an internal "photo album" of emotionally resonant images that we can refer to when the need arises. Take some time to discover whatever images feel potent to you, images that help you readily connect with a positive feeling—be it tenderness, love, compassion, or joy—anything that makes you feel better, that shifts your emotional state. You might try recalling a happy moment shared with a friend, imagining being enveloped in a loving embrace, or picturing yourself in a place that is warm and serene. You could visualize a helpful person or group of people assisting you with your fear, and then let yourself feel the presence of their love and support. Or you could try practicing compassion for yourself. For instance, you could imagine your adult self comforting the scared child within you, giving your child self what he or she needs to be no longer afraid and then letting yourself feel the empathy and love.

Figuring out what works best for you may take some time. That's why it's better to experiment with visualization before you're feeling anxious. If images and positive feelings don't readily come to you, don't worry or get frustrated. Like any of the anxiety-regulating techniques in this chapter, visualization is a skill that you can develop. It just takes some time and a little bit of effort. With practice, you can learn how to generate positive feelings through visualization and use these emotions to neutralize your fear. You can use the Positive Imagery Tool to help ease your distress.

Positive Imagery Tool

When you notice feeling anxious or afraid, take the following steps:

1. Acknowledge your discomfort.
2. Call to mind images, memories, or situations that evoke positive feelings.
3. Focus in on this material as you breathe deeply.
4. Imagine the positive feelings washing over you and neutralizing your anxiety or fear.
5. When your anxiety or fear sufficiently melts away, take a moment to sit with and appreciate what you're feeling.

TAKE HEART

Here's one last calming strategy that can help tame fear.

Neuroscientist Steven W. Porges suggests that there may be a very simple way to counter stress and calm our nerves.[10] The key to this strategy is the vagus nerve, which is the main channel of the parasympathetic branch of the nervous system. The vagus nerve originates in the brain stem and carries signals to various parts of the body, including the heart, lungs, and intestines. It's closely involved with regulating our heart rate and breathing.

Heart Tool

When you're feeling anxious or fearful, take the following steps:

1. Place one hand in the center of your chest over your heart and breathe deeply from your abdomen.
2. Call to mind moments of serenity or joy and amplify them in your imagination until you can feel their energy in every cell of your body.
3. When you feel relaxed, take a moment to sit with and appreciate this new place.

Activation of the vagus nerve calms our fear response; it slows down heart rate, decreases blood pressure, and promotes an overall state of relaxation. Simply placing a hand in the center of your chest over your heart can stimulate the vagus nerve and soothe the rhythms of your heart. This strategy may be especially effective if you combine it with deep breathing and visualization. You can use the Heart Tool to help manage any anxiety you encounter as you open up to your feelings.

YOUR TURN

In my own efforts to tame my fear, I've used each and every one of the strategies I've shared with you in this chapter, and they've served me well. I teach them to my clients every day, and they make use of them with great success. As they are more able to face their fear instead of run from it, and to respond to it in a way that helps ease their distress, they feel more in control and more able to take a look at what's going on for them emotionally. Now you have a tool kit that you can draw from as you begin to open up to your feelings.

It's important to remember that the techniques in this chapter are skills that you can develop through practice. Although they're meant to be used in the moment when you're getting close to your feelings and starting to feel anxious or afraid, I recommend practicing them whenever you can. Think of them as exercises you would do to get your body in shape or to stay physically fit, except that in this case you're working on your anxiety-regulating muscles. Each time you practice, you're developing your capacity to manage your distress and gain control over your fear. Each time you practice, you get better at it. And by responding to your feelings in this way, you're changing your brain's response to your emotions. Instead of responding with fear, you'll come to perceive your feelings as something you can handle and don't need to be afraid of.

Now, it's important to acknowledge that you may not be able to eliminate all of your anxiety. That's okay. Remember, anxiety is a helpful signal that something is going on inside you that needs attention. In this way, it's your friend. You need that information. Further, a little anxiety is not a bad thing, as it prompts you not to be complacent. You need it to motivate you to move forward and get the life you really want. That being said, however, unwarranted anxiety or fear that stops you in your tracks is not a good thing. It's this kind of distress that you need to be able to handle. Your main goal is to be able to reduce discomfort to a manageable level so that you're able to remain open to your feelings. The strategies covered in this chapter are intended to help you do just that. Give them each a try and get to know what works best for you.

CHAPTER TAKE-HOME POINTS

- Anxiety or fear can be a helpful sign that we're getting closer to our emotions.
- We can reduce our discomfort to a manageable level so that our emotions don't have to feel overwhelming.
- Identifying and simply naming our feelings decreases anxiety.
- Describing and tracking the physical manifestations of anxiety or fear can regulate our emotional experience.
- Abdominal breathing stimulates our parasympathetic nervous system and calms our fear response.
- Visualization and the positive feelings it engenders can act as an antidote to anxiety and fear.
- Placing a hand on your heart stimulates the vagus nerve, which calms your nervous system.
- Practicing these strategies increases your capacity to manage your distress and get control over your fear.

CHAPTER 6

Step Three
Feeling It Through

I'm not afraid of storms for I'm learning how to sail my ship.

—Louisa May Alcott

Brian, a schoolteacher in his mid-thirties, struggled to tell me about a strained encounter he had with his parents over the weekend that had left him feeling disconnected and numb.

"What's coming up?" I asked softly, noticing that his eyes had become teary. "What are you feeling now?"

Brian looked down and focused inward. He sat quietly, then looked up at me and said, "Um . . . I guess it's a combination of hurt and anger. Yeah, that's it. I'm hurt by what they did and angry. But mostly I'm feeling frustrated with myself for not being able to let my feelings out. I know what I'm feeling, I know what's there, but something blocks it. Something anchors me down."

I knew that these kinds of frustrations were what had brought Brian to my office to begin with. He had described feeling "weighed down"—an understandable consequence of growing up in a family that had little tolerance for emotion. Whether it was excitement or pride, anger or sadness, happiness or love, Brian's emotional expression had often been met with distance and disdain. As a result, he had learned to doubt his feelings, to suppress and deny them, and ended up feeling depressed and lifeless. But as we worked together, I could see that he was coming alive emotionally.

Brian continued, "It's like . . . sometimes when I'm going for a run, I'll have these conversations in my head where I imagine talking to my parents, telling them how I feel. It'll seem as though I'm starting to let my feelings out. But then I'll get to the end of my run and realize that I haven't. Nothing's changed. I don't feel any different. I think, *What's the use? It's just not worth it.*"

As is so often the case, Brian was thinking about what he would say to his parents rather than just letting himself feel what he was feeling in the moment. I thought for a second about pointing this out to him, but then reminded myself that we needed to get back to whatever it was that was bringing tears to his eyes. We needed to get back to his feelings.

"That's painful to me, Brian," I said empathically, "that you would give up on yourself. That you would feel like throwing in the towel. It's painful for me to think about you feeling that way."

Brian nodded but seemed taken aback, unsure of what to make of this direct expression of care. His lips moved as though he were about to say something, but nothing came out. He tried again once more and then said, "It's painful to me as well. I mean . . . thank you . . . um . . ." Another pause, then, "I think that if I could just . . ."

Before Brian could veer off into his thoughts, I stopped him. "Brian, what are you noticing inside as you sit with this?" I asked.

He listened for a moment and then said, "Um . . . it's a warm feeling . . . in my chest." He looked to the side and sat very still. Then he shifted in his chair and sat up, as though he were trying to shake himself off and rise above whatever feelings were nearing the surface.

"Brian, just try to stay present with what you're feeling. What all is there?"

"Well," he tried to be matter-of-fact as he referred to my empathy for him, "not a lot of people say that to you. It's a nice thing to say." He paused, then shook his head. "I just don't understand why my parents couldn't say nice things to me. Why did they always have to be . . . focus on my shortcomings, or . . . " He stopped, closed his eyes.

"It's all right," I said. "Just let the feelings come."

With innocent eyes, he looked at me and said, "I feel like a little kid . . . and I remember coming home from an awards ceremony at school. I had all these awards, and my parents had nothing to say to me. They said nothing . . . about . . . it . . . And I just remember . . . in my bedroom . . . sitting . . ."

His head fell forward and his shoulders began to shake as waves of sorrow, one after the other, washed over him. I encouraged him to breathe, let the feelings move through him, and remain present to his pain.

After a minute or two, the tide began to recede.

The storm finally over, the waters now calm, Brian sat in the stillness and sighed. He looked up at me and said, "This is so what's been holding me down."

"Not anymore, Brian," I said. "Not anymore."

THE NATURE OF THINGS

Brian is learning to be present with his feelings and open up to the experience so that he can heal the sorrow and pain he's carried around for far too long. When we truly feel our feelings, we free up a wellspring of energy inside us. When this emotional energy is allowed to flow in the way that nature intended, it carries us to a place of wholeness and renewal. And even when emotions are painful, allowing ourselves to feel our feelings is healing in and of itself.[1] Opening ourselves up to emotional experience increases our aliveness and vitality, brings us a sense of clarity and meaning, and connects us to a deeper, fuller experience of ourselves. Further, it's empowering to face and master what we have avoided or feared.

But fear can get in the way. It can prevent us from discovering the simple truth that when fully felt, feelings don't last forever, no matter how intense they may seem in the moment. Like an ocean wave, they start off small, rise up in intensity until they crest, and then dissipate. They can come and go rather quickly or take some time to resolve. Several waves of emotion can come in succession, or one solitary wave can rise and fall on its own.

By acknowledging and staying with our emotions rather than blocking them or pushing them away, we can learn to tolerate them and see them through.

Learning how to be with our feelings is like learning how to sail. Sometimes the waters are rough and difficult to maneuver; sometimes they're calm. Sometimes the current is strong and intense; sometimes it flows more gently. Sometimes the sea is predictable, and sometimes it can change dramatically and unexpectedly. Navigating these different conditions can feel scary, but the more we do it, the easier it becomes and the better we feel. With practice we can master the skills needed to sail our emotional ship.

LET THE RIVER RUN

Oftentimes when my clients are on the brink of an emotional experience—their feelings right there, ready to break through—they will stop and ask me, "What do I do now?" They find themselves in uncharted waters, unsure of which direction to go and anxious about how to get there. Like many of us, they desperately want to be in control.

But when it comes to experiencing feelings, being in control or taking action is not what's needed. It's about being open to and making room for an experience and then allowing a process to unfold.

More than anything else, we need to get out of our own way. Too often, we interrupt the process and stop our feelings before they fully arrive. For example, we start to feel happy and quickly shut the door on it. We begin to feel sad and then brush it off. Or we become angry and start questioning our response.

Here is where emotional mindfulness can again be so useful to us. It can help us make room for and embrace the richness of our feelings and feel our way through them. In particular, six different elements of emotional mindfulness can aid us in our efforts to experience our emotions fully. They are

1. Acceptance
2. Paying attention
3. Slowing down
4. Giving way

5. Seeing it through
6. Reflecting

The rest of this chapter is devoted to helping you learn how to cultivate each of these elements so that you can stay present to your feelings all the way through to completion. With repeated practice you'll develop your ability to manage and make good use of your emotional experience.

IT IS WHAT IT IS

"I'm fine," Brian answered when I asked him how he'd been since we last saw each other.

"Really?" I asked, not quite convinced. "You don't look fine."

Brian admitted that for the last few days he'd been out of sorts. He'd had a phone conversation with his mother that had left him feeling irritated and unsettled because of her tendency to be patronizing and judgmental toward him. It was not uncommon for her behavior to bother Brian, but this time she had made a comment that Brian found downright demeaning. I asked, "When you think about what your mother said, how do you feel toward her?"

"Well, you know, this is nothing new," he answered. "She does this kind of thing all the time. What am I going to do? I mean, it's not like she's going to change."

Brian was rationalizing, getting ahead of himself, and not allowing his feelings to come to the fore. "That may be true," I said. "But it doesn't tell us how you feel toward her when she acts this way."

"Well, it bothers me," he began to admit.

"I'm sure it does, but 'bothers' is a little vague. Can you be more specific about how you feel?"

"Um, it makes me angry, I guess."

Brian seemed to be hesitating. I asked, "You're not sure?"

"No . . . I mean, yeah, it makes me angry. She can be so hateful."

"Of course you're angry. That makes total sense," I paused. "What's that like?" I asked, hoping that he'd allow himself to begin to feel his way through what was inside.

He looked at me and then said, "You know, for a second I feel like I could get worked up, but then I feel kind of bad. I mean,

I don't think she realizes what she's doing. So it's not really fair of me to get angry if she doesn't know any better. Is it?"

ACCEPTING WHAT IS

Brian was starting to judge himself. Just as his anger was beginning to arrive on the scene, he interrupted it by questioning whether it was a valid response, especially toward his mother.

This dilemma is not uncommon. Many of us feel uncomfortable about having negative feelings toward a loved one. We think that if we allow the negative feelings to come out that somehow they will cancel out all the positive feelings. But they don't. Multiple feelings can and do coexist. And as we all know, sometimes it's the people who are most dear to us who can make us the angriest.

For Brian to work through his feelings and get to a different place, he needed to first *accept* what he feels.

Acceptance is one of the basic principles of mindfulness. It is an unconditional attitude, a way of seeing things free of judgment, criticism, or intention to change. An attitude of acceptance can free us up to more fully experience our emotions as they occur.

We need to be willing to see and accept our feelings for what they are. If we're angry, we're angry. If we're sad, we're sad. And if we're happy, we're happy. Our experience is neither right nor wrong—it simply is. When we don't accept what we're feeling, we can't engage with it or do anything about it. Our feelings aren't able to flow, and we end up stuck. As psychologist and York University professor Leslie Greenberg explains, we have to be willing to first let our feelings "arrive" before we can go anywhere else.[2]

Feelings are a little bit like the weather. We have no choice about what it's going to be like outside, and we can't change it. We can't will the sun to shine or the rain to fall or the snow to stop. But if we're patient and wait long enough, the weather will change (especially here in Minnesota, where the weather can change on a dime!). If we fight it, if we agonize about the cold or complain about the rain, we just makes things worse. When we can accept the weather for what it is, we can deal with it and move on. The same can be said about our feelings. We don't choose our feelings, and fighting them won't make them go away. We don't have to like them, but if we can accept our feelings for what they are and allow them to have some space, we can then begin to feel our way through to a different and better place.

Although the tendency to criticize or judge our feelings may seem formidable, acceptance can be a powerful antidote. It can free us from the chatter of our thoughts and allow us to make contact with our authentic self. Although this may seem a case of "easier said than done," allowing ourselves to get curious and befriend and accept our feelings opens up the natural flow of our emotions and enables the process of change to begin. We just need to be willing and motivated to give it a try.

Here are some suggestions to help you stay open to your emotional experience and be more accepting of your feelings.

Practicing Acceptance

- If you notice yourself trying to avoid your feelings or feeling conflicted about them, give yourself permission to see them simply for what they are.
- Remind yourself to put judgment or questioning aside and instead to practice getting curious about your feelings.
- If you find yourself feeling conflicted about your feelings, remind yourself that emotions are neither right nor wrong; they just are. Then take a look and see what's there.
- Notice if there's any resistance in your body; if there is, breathe into it, allowing the energy to open up and flow. Gently encourage yourself to stay open.

GETTING IN TOUCH

Brian admitted that he felt conflicted about his anger toward his mother, but could also see how denying his feelings wasn't getting him anywhere. In fact, it was just making things worse. He felt anxious and stuck. Brian recognized that he needed to try something different.

"I know it feels scary to you," I said, "but I wonder if, for a moment, you'd be willing to give yourself permission to feel your feelings, to honor whatever is there for you. That's really the only way you're going to get to the other side of this. Would you be willing to do that?"

He thought about it for a moment, shrugged, and then said, "Well, I suppose it can't be worse than what I *have* been feeling."

"Actually, I'm convinced you'll be much better off," I said. "You just need to give it a try. Are you willing to take a look at this anger of yours?"

"Yeah," he replied, "but . . . I'm not sure how to do that."

"Let me give you a hand," I said. "First, why don't you try sitting up. It'll help you be more in touch with what's happening inside you." Brian placed his feet flat on the floor, shifted in his chair as he sat up straight, then looked at me for what to do next. "Now let yourself recall the conversation you had with your mother. Picture yourself on the phone with her. Hear her voice and the comment she made." He sat very still for a moment, focusing inward, his face intent and serious. Then his bottom lip began to curl inward. The interaction with his mother was coming back to him along with his anger.

"As you get in touch with your feelings, what do you notice inside you?" I asked.

He looked up at me, eyes narrowed, and said, "I'm feeling kind of irritated."

"I can see that. Let's give that some room. Can you describe for me what that feels like?"

He thought about it for a moment and then said, "I don't know."

This was new territory for Brian, so I said to him, "Tune in to your body and just describe what you notice going on inside you."

He listened for a bit and then said, "Um, I feel sort of tense."

"Where exactly in your body are you feeling that?"

"In my chest."

"Okay. Now concentrate on that place. Don't try to make anything happen. Just notice that tension and let's see what comes."

Brian looked down, focusing on his body. He moved his shoulders back and forth, then looked up at me and said, "It starts to open up a bit."

By focusing on his experience, Brian was making room inside himself for his feelings, and the energy of his anger was beginning to move. Just then, the color in Brian's face changed. "What else do you notice?" I asked.

"I'm feeling warm. My skin feels hot."

Sounds like anger to me, I thought to myself and then said, "Let yourself be with that." I waited and then asked, "What else is there?"

He rested his forehead on the tip of one hand, sat for a moment, and then shook his head. "Now I'm starting to think about it. I'm going off into my thoughts." Through our work, Brian was becoming better at recognizing when he started to think about things and lose contact with his feelings.

"Just let the thoughts fall away. Don't give them any power. Focus back on the physical sensations and see where they go. What else do you notice?"

Brian focused inward again. After a moment his eyebrows lifted and he looked startled. "Wow . . . I feel all this energy inside me, rising up. That's strange."

PAYING ATTENTION

Not strange at all, actually. Brian's experience is a great example of what can happen when we pay attention to our felt experience. It opens up.

As we learned in Chapter Three, emotions are felt in the body. If we didn't have a body, we wouldn't have feelings—there'd be no place to feel them. Focusing on physical sensations helps us connect with our feelings. As Brian listens to what's going on inside him, as he pays attention to his physical experience, his anger becomes more palpable and able to move.

The word *emotion* derives from the Latin *emovere,* which essentially means "to move out or away." Healthy feelings do just that. Whether it's a gentle flowing sensation or a rush of energy, emotions move. They are often experienced as moving from the inside out, starting in the torso and progressing outward toward our extremities.[3] For instance,

- With anger there's an upward surge of energy (for example, blood rushing to your face, a tingling sensation in your arms).
- With sadness there's a welling up of tears.

- With happiness and love there's a flowing of warmth from the chest throughout the torso.
- Although fear can cause us to freeze, its energy can also flow outward to our feet, readying us to flee.

Guilt and shame are a little different. The energetic flow of these emotions runs in the other direction, from the outside in, causing us to want to pull inward and hide. But whatever their "direction," when you learn to notice them, you'll find that emotions are always moving.

Mindfully paying attention to the physical experience of emotion creates an internal space in which our feelings can come forward and run their course. In Brian's case, as he focuses on what's going on inside him, he's making room for his anger to be realized. It first shows up as a vague sense of irritability that on further inspection manifests as tension in his chest. As he concentrates on this tension, it opens up and gives way to anger, which manifests as warmth as his body heat increases. As he stays with this feeling, he experiences a surge of energy as his anger releases.

Paying attention to feelings doesn't require anything more. We don't need to make anything happen; we're not responsible for figuring anything out. All we have to do is stay present and observe. Cultivating this way of being with ourselves is similar to the practice of attending to the breath in mindfulness meditation. As anyone who has practiced meditation knows, focusing on our breathing has the interesting effect of both narrowing our range of attention while simultaneously heightening our level of awareness and engagement. When we focus in on and pay attention to our feelings, the same thing happens. Our awareness of the subtleties of our emotions increases, and our experience deepens.

Paying attention in this way takes some practice. It's easy to get distracted, worry about the past or future, or jump into problem-solving mode. When you catch yourself doing this sort of thing (just as Brian did when he recognized that he was veering off into his thoughts), simply redirect your attention to your felt experience. Whatever it is that's there, focus on it and observe what happens. If you get lost traveling down a road of associations, bring yourself back to whatever it was that prompted an emotional reaction in the first place. Whether it was a hurtful comment someone made, a loving moment, or a goal you finally reached, visualize the experience, hear it, touch it, taste it, and then stay present with what comes.

Here is a summary of the previous suggestions to help you focus on your felt experience.

Paying Attention

- Get quiet and tune in to what's going on inside you.
- Locate the experience in your body and concentrate on that place.
- Don't try to make anything happen; just watch, listen, and observe.
- When your attention wanders, remind yourself to come back to your felt experience.

ONE STEP AT A TIME

"Looks like there's a lot going on inside, Brian," I said.

"Yeah, it feels kind of overwhelming," he admitted, with an anxious look on his face.

"Let's slow down and take this one step at a time." Brian sighed and seemed a little relieved. I continued, "First, tell me more about this energy."

"Well . . . I feel . . . like I want to yell," he admitted.

"You mean you want to retaliate verbally?" I asked.

"Yeah, like I want to tell my mother off."

"I can understand wanting to do that," I said, "but *experiencing* your anger isn't about putting it into words, not yet at least. It's about really letting yourself physically feel all of what's inside you." I waited a moment for that to sink in and then suggested, "Let's just try to stay present with what's going on inside you. What wants to happen in your body right now?"

He tuned in to his experience again and said, "I don't know. It's like I have all this energy building up inside."

"Where does it want to go?"

"I feel like I need to *do* something." As he said this, Brian moved his hands in front of him as though he were forcefully pushing something out of his way.

"Okay, let's stop and look at this. What's going on with your hands?"

Brian looked at his hands for a moment as though he were discovering something he didn't know was there. "They're tingling," he said.

"As you stay with that sensation, what wants to happen?" I asked.

"I . . . I feel like . . . like I could lash out." Suddenly he looked worried, and asserted, "But I would *never* do that. I'm not a violent person."

"I know you're not. That's not a concern. I'm more concerned about you allowing yourself to have a full experience of your feelings."

Like many people, Brian felt uncomfortable with the impulses that can arise with anger, but his urge to lash out made complete physiological sense—it's the "fight" side of the fight-or-flight response deeply wired into our system, there to mobilize us against harm or attack. Our goal with any emotion is not to be reactive but to learn how to *tolerate* it, to slow down and feel our way through the internal experience. This is especially true when it comes to anger.

I explained the "wired-in" aspect of his response to Brian and then added, "What we're trying to do here is make plenty of room for your feelings. We're not talking about what you would do in real life. Of course you'd never be aggressive; that wouldn't be okay. But being able to tolerate your feelings, to ride out all that's inside you, is essential to your being able to make use of your anger in a positive way. The flip side of it is that you remain powerless."

"Well, I don't want that," he said, looking more determined.

"Okay then," I said, nodding my head, and then waited a moment for his sense of resolve to solidly take hold. "Now, if you come back to that instance with your mother and stay very close to what's inside you, can you let yourself give way to all that's there?"

Brian looked to the side and focused inward. He seemed very close to his emotions. He sat still for a moment and then looked back at me and said, "I'm not sure what to do. I mean, its right there, I can feel it, but . . ."

"Just notice what's there," I said. "Take a deep breath and, as you exhale, let yourself give in to the experience and ride it out. Open yourself up and just let whatever comes come."

He took a breath and let it out. Something seemed to release. He sat with it for a moment and then looked at me, face flushed, and said, "Wow—it feels like all this energy came rushing out of me in a big blast."

SLOWING DOWN

Had Brian relied on his usual way of doing things—mindlessly running over his emotions—his experience would have been at best superficial and unproductive. His anger would have remained partially buried and would have continued to fester. But by slowing down and taking things one step at a time, he's feeling his way through to the other side.

Emotions are multifaceted and need time to be experienced in their entirety. When we rush through them—our default tendency—we miss the subtleties of our feelings. We need to *feel* our emotions in all their complexity in order for them to be of benefit to us.

It's amazing how slowing down in the moment enables us to be more present with our emotional experience. Slowing down helps us by

- Decreasing our anxiety
- Bringing us more fully into the present moment
- Making it easier for us to notice the nuances of our feelings
- Breaking up our emotional experience into smaller, more workable pieces
- Expanding and deepening our experience of our feelings

By slowing down, Brian is cultivating an aspect of mindfulness called *participatory observation*. He's both watching his emotions and physical sensations and experiencing them at the same time. First, he becomes aware of energy building up inside. Next, he notices a desire to retaliate verbally, which is followed by an urge to do something. When he looks more closely, he senses that his hands are tingling, and as he examines them he also feels an urge to lash out. Finally, as he sits with his experience, he notices and feels an explosive rush of energy. Engaging in this way heightens

Brian's awareness of his anger and its different dimensions and allows his anger to become more fully embodied. At the same time, the experience of his anger changes from something that seems overwhelming to a moment-to-moment process that unfolds in manageable steps.

Sometimes it helps to see your feelings as if you were watching a movie or film, where you can slow down the action and experience an emotion "frame by frame." For instance, you begin by visualizing an experience and then slowly play it out in your mind's eye, exploring feelings a little at a time as they come up. At any moment, you can hit the pause button, stop the film, and spend some time in a particular place. In this way you can slow down the experience, sit with your feelings, and give them all the room they need, and then move on when you feel ready.

Here are some other suggestions to help you slow down and stay present with your feelings.

Slowing Down

- Take time to feel the complexity of your feelings, to notice and experience each dimension (the texture, the breadth, the depth, the intensity, and so on).
- Focus on the feeling and ask it what it wants to do, where it wants to go. Stay present and *wait* to see what comes.
- Whenever your attention wanders or you jump ahead, reorient yourself to your present emotional experience and sit with it.

GIVING WAY

I have many fond memories of childhood family vacations spent at the Jersey Shore. It was my favorite part of the summer—the smell of the sea, the sound of the seagulls, walking barefoot in the sand. My sisters and I would spend most of our days playing in the ocean. We'd walk out just far enough until we were lifted up, buoyed by the water, and float up and down on the rolling sea waiting for "a big one." Sure enough, a wave would come. We'd spy it out in the distance, growing in size as it headed our way. In that moment, we knew that all we could do was go with it, let ourselves be pulled upward in the swell, and ride it out to the shore. Sure, it was a little scary. But mostly it was exhilarating.

Sometimes, when we slow down and stay present, our feelings gently come into our awareness like the ebbing of the tide. At other times, they build in intensity inside us and rise up like a "big one" headed for the shoreline. It's in these moments that it's often best to *give way* to the experience, open up and be receptive to the flow, and ride the wave. Our sorrow rises up and we give way to the pain, our joy rises up and we give way to elation, or, as in Brian's case, our anger rises up and we give way to the rush of energy inside us. It can be a little scary, but it doesn't need to be. After all, no one has ever drowned from riding the waves of his or her feelings. And, more important, the experience is filled with the potential of better things to come.

Giving way has a quality of openness. Rather than steeling ourselves or white-knuckling our way through our feelings, we're *softening* into them, letting them wash over us and move through us. When you feel the energy of your emotions rising inside you, gently encourage yourself to go with the experience. Take a deep breath and, as you exhale, allow the energy of your feelings to flow. Visualize yourself in an open stance with your arms spread wide as you welcome the feelings. Feel them come to you. Let them fill the space you've created.

When the feelings are difficult or overwhelming, it can also help to have the support of a trusted friend or loved one, someone

---

Giving Way

- As the energy rises in you, encourage the feeling to emerge. Say to yourself, *Just let the feelings come,* or simply *Let it come.*
- Breathe deeply into the feeling, allowing it to wash over you or move through you.
- Imagine yourself softening or relaxing into the feeling and then let yourself do just that.
- Remember to breathe and stay open as you're going with the flow of your feelings.

---

who can be there for you and help you manage the experience. Of course, it needs to be someone with whom you feel safe and comfortable being very open.

On the preceding page are some guidelines to help you open up and give way to your feelings.

A WORD (OR TWO) ABOUT ANGER

When Brian gets in touch with his anger, he feels the energy of it rumbling inside him, experiences an impulse to lash out, and rides out a blast of emotion. All of this happens without his leaving his chair. Emotional experience is on the inside, but expressing our feelings is something different. It happens on the outside (and is the subject of the next chapter).

When I talk to people about needing to learn how to fully experience their feelings, invariably someone inquires about whether anger is an exception. Anger is a feeling like any other, but as this question suggests, it's one that continues to be misunderstood.

Many of us have mistakenly equated anger with unhealthy, destructive behavior. For some, the mere mention of the word "anger" calls to mind images of yelling, hitting, breaking things, and so on. *How would that be helpful?* people wonder, and rightly so. These and other aggressive behaviors are not about experiencing a feeling. They're attempts to discharge anger by taking it out on something or someone, otherwise known as "acting out." Behaving in this way is reactive—it's as though there's no space inside for the feeling to be tolerated and contained, so it has to be expressed externally. It's also misguided because it does little to nothing to dispel the anger. In fact, research has repeatedly shown that "venting" anger (for example, screaming, pounding a pillow, or lashing out at someone) only intensifies and prolongs the feeling.[4] In short, it makes us angrier.

Learning to tolerate anger inside us, to mindfully feel our way through it to a different place as Brian is doing, increases our mastery of the feeling and empowers us to be able to use it in a productive way. As Zen master Thich Nhat Hanh wisely encourages, "Accept your anger because you know, you understand, that you can take care of it; you can transform it into positive energy."[5]

RIDING OUT THE WAVE

"A big blast, huh? Sounds intense. What's that like?" I asked, wanting Brian to fully experience his anger.

"I can feel it moving through me," he said. "There's a lot of heat."

"Just stay with that and let it flow."

Brian sat quietly, focusing inward, giving his anger lots of room. I wondered where his mother was in all of this. After all, it was the interaction with her that gave rise to these feelings. It would be important for Brian to experience them in relation to her. "Brian, you were recalling being on the phone with your mother when these feelings started to emerge. How do you imagine she'd react to this blast of anger?"

He paused for a moment and then said, "I see her reeling back with this surprised look on her face."

"What's that like?"

Brian paused for a moment, checked in with himself, and then said, "It feels . . . empowering." He sighed and then sat up straight. "I'm tired of her getting the best of me. I'm not going to put up with it anymore."

This attitude was very different. By opening up to his anger, Brian was uncovering a sense of strength and clarity that had heretofore eluded him. It was crucial that Brian fully feel this new way of being so that he would be able to carry it forward into his life. With that in mind I asked him, "What does that feel like inside you?"

"I feel bigger, and she's a lot smaller. She feels less threatening," he said, appearing rather pleased.

I could see that. Brian was sitting up straight, his chest open and his face clear—a marked contrast to how he looked at the beginning of the session.

"That's impressive," I said. "Your mother has loomed so *large* in your psyche for a long, long time."

"Tell me about it!" He sighed again. "What a relief."

Brian had arrived at the other side of his wave of anger. I said, "That's so great. Just let yourself really feel that sense of relief. Breathe into it and really savor it."

We sat together in this place for a moment, taking it in. But it then looked like something else was stirring in Brian. I asked him what he was becoming aware of.

"Actually, I'm feeling sad now too."

"Yeah, I can see that. Just let it come, Brian. It's part of your experience as well."

"I mean. My mother can be so difficult at times . . . and I'm relieved that I can let myself feel angry with her, but . . . ," he said, as his eyes filled up with tears. "Underneath it all . . . what I really want from her . . . is her love."

SEEING IT THROUGH

Brian is experiencing the transforming power of his emotions. By staying with his anger and seeing it through to completion, he arrives at a new and different place. No longer crippled by his fear or feeling hopeless, he feels empowered and determined to stand up for himself.

When we're able to stay with our emotions and really give them their due, they put us in touch with a wealth of internal resources. As psychiatrist and Georgetown University professor Norman Rosenthal describes in his book *The Emotional Revolution,* our emotions bring us "gifts."[6] For instance, fear brings us the gift of wisdom, sadness brings us healing, guilt brings remorse, shame gives us humility, happiness leads to growth, and love brings us closeness and connection. And, as Brian is discovering, anger brings us clarity and strength. All these gifts allow us to move forward in a healthy way.

We can't, however, benefit from these gifts if we start to feel our feelings and then back away from them. Only partially experiencing them is not enough; we need to get on board and ride the wave all the way to the shore.

But how do we know when we've gone the distance?

When we feel our feelings all the way through to completion, we experience an internal body shift. It may be marked or it may be subtle, but on some level we feel freed up, or, as Brian did, we feel relieved. Our emotions are no longer fighting to be heard, we're no longer working to fend them off, and the energy inside us is allowed to run its natural course. In the wake of fully experiencing our true feelings—whether it is of anger, joy, sadness, fear, guilt, shame, or love—a shift takes place inside, our body eases up, and we feel better, lighter. And, having arrived at our emotional core, we experience a sense of personal truth. Even if the experience was difficult or unpleasant, our emotions feel right, and we know that we're doing or have done what we needed to do.

If, after trying for some time to work through your feelings, you're still feeling unsettled or you haven't experienced a shift, it's possible that there's more emotion that needs to be processed. As psychologist and philosopher Eugene Gendlin wrote in his book *Focusing*, "Nothing that feels bad is ever the last step."[7] It's an indication that you need to go further.

When you're feeling stuck and there's little to no emotional movement, it's possible that the feelings you've been focused on are actually defensive and are masking underlying core emotions. Try putting aside the more apparent feelings for a moment and see if you can sense what other feelings might be hidden underneath. When you're able to make contact with your core feelings, they should open up and begin to flow. You can then see them through the rest of the way.

Another possibility when your feelings don't readily shift or change is that they may have roots that go back to a much earlier time. They may link to unresolved feelings from the past that also need to be uncovered, processed, and healed. For example, the sadness that Brian was experiencing (described earlier in the chapter) had roots that went all the way back to his childhood. As he struggled to contain the feelings stirring inside him, a childhood memory was unlocked—coming home from a school awards ceremony to parents who were unresponsive and emotionally absent—which opened the door to a wellspring of buried emotion and allowed the process of healing to begin. If the feelings you're focusing on seem old, familiar, or not quite matched to the current situation, try this. While staying connected to your visceral experience, let yourself drift back in time to when you first felt the same way. Use the current feeling as a "bridge" to the past.[8] As you turn inward, notice whatever memories, sensations, and additional feelings arise, and try to stay present. Your feelings will likely start to move, and you can begin the work of seeing them through to a place of healing and renewal.

Sometimes when we feel our way through one emotion, we find out that there are others there as well. As Brian discovered after riding out his anger, he also felt sad. He was hurt by his mother's critical behavior and pained by her inability to be open and loving. By allowing himself to feel and explore his anger, Brian was then able to acknowledge his sadness and allow himself to grieve. After working through his sadness, it's possible that Brian might discover loving feelings as well. Such is the complexity of our emotional experience.

Here are some suggestions to help you see your feelings through.

Seeing Your Feelings Through

- Encourage yourself to stay with your feelings, to remain open and allow the experience to come to full fruition.
- Keep coming back to the feeling—spending time with it, allowing it to unfold—until you sense that it has run its course.
- If the feelings seem familiar or old, try using them as a bridge. While remaining connected to your emotional experience, let yourself drift back in time and see if you can uncover their source. Try to stay open to whatever memories, sensations, and additional feelings arise.
- Check in with yourself, go inside and listen, sense what else is there. Ask yourself, *Is that all? Is there more? What else is there?* and let it come.

TAKE TIME TO REFLECT

Having fully ridden out the waves of his emotions—his anger and his sadness—Brian then needed to take some time to reflect on his experience, to step back and take a look at what he'd done, what it was like for him, and what he had learned. He talked about how it was hard for him to face his anger, that it felt a little scary, but that it also felt right. He could see more clearly just how much his childhood experience had led him to be emotionally constricted, but he could also see how, by facing his fears, he was changing. He went on to say,

The more we do this, the more I see just how much I've been holding back, how afraid I've been of having my feelings. I didn't realize how much I'd been carrying around—how much I'd been pushing my feelings back, stuffing what I felt. I guess I thought that was somehow going to make me feel more in control. But it didn't. Actually it did just the opposite. I feel more in control now than I did before. Letting myself feel angry, just letting it all come out, wasn't necessarily easy, but it feels freeing. And I feel kind of proud of myself for doing it, for not letting fear hold me back anymore. It also makes me feel hopeful that I *can* do this. That I don't have to feel weighed down anymore. That if I keep working at it, I can feel strong enough to be myself, that my life can be better.

Reflecting on our experience and acknowledging what we've done are essential parts of the process. They help us really appreciate the magnitude of what we've done—that we're facing our fears and are turning things around, that we're freeing ourselves up to have a better life. Reflection allows us to honor this new and different way of being and more fully assimilate it into our sense of self. And when we stop to acknowledge our progress, it makes us feel good.

In terms of the way our brain works, reflection gets the "making sense" function of the left brain involved in our process. Just as insight alone is not enough to bring about lasting change, neither is experience without understanding. The left brain helps us understand and make sense of our experience. For instance,

Reflecting

- Find a quiet place and reflect on your experience. Let yourself step back and view it in its entirety.
- Think about what you've done, what experiencing your feelings was like, how it came to be.
- Contrast how you were feeling before with how you're feeling now. Note any changes (for example, what you sense in your body, what you think about yourself, and so on).
- Write in a journal about your experiences and what you're learning about yourself.

as we reflect on what we did, we might think to ourselves, *I was so afraid of my feelings and was doing all these things to avoid them. But when I slowed myself down and stayed present with them, it wasn't as bad as I thought it would be. I'm learning that I can do this, that I can handle my feelings.* Reflecting on our experience in this way brings right-brain (emotional experience) and left-brain (understanding) processes together and facilitates the development of new neural connections.[9] It's the "top" part of our bottom-up process that helps rewire our brain.

Simply spending some time reflecting on and making sense of experience takes such little effort but has powerful effects. On the preceding page are some suggestions to help you reflect on your experience.

TAKING CARE

Our feelings need care, and care takes time. When we care for our feelings, we stay with them and give them the room and attention they need. We acknowledge their presence, slow down, and open ourselves up to experience them in their fullness.

Imagine watching an emotionally powerful movie. You settle into your seat in the theater still slightly distracted, still caught up in the details of your life. Then, shortly after the movie begins, time seems to slow down, the past and future fall away, and you come more fully to what you're seeing on the screen. You find yourself really paying attention, getting actively involved and caring for the characters. You feel fear when there's danger, joy when there's success, touched when there's tenderness, and sorrow when there's pain. The movie doesn't happen in an instant; it takes time—it plays out frame by frame, scene by scene. But as you stay with it and give yourself over to the experience, you're taken along on a rich and moving journey.

The same thing can happen in our life. When we give our feelings their due, when we honor our experience and fully see it through, we transform our feelings into positive energy. But even though experiencing our feelings is personally gratifying and, at times, adequate, often we'd like to be able to share them with others. In fact, emotions prompt us to do just that. In the next chapter, we're going to look at how we can more easily express our feelings and use them to connect and get closer to others.

CHAPTER TAKE-HOME POINTS

- When fully felt, feelings don't last forever. They have a beginning, middle, and end.
- We need to be willing to see and accept our feelings for what they are.
- Attuning to what's going on inside us frees up the energy of our emotions and allows that energy to move.
- Emotions are multifaceted. We need to feel them in all their complexity in order for them to be of benefit to us.
- There comes a moment when it's often best simply to "give way" to our feelings.
- Experiencing our feelings and expressing our feelings are two different things.
- When we stay open to our feelings and really give them their due, they bring us a wealth of internal resources.
- When we feel our emotions through to completion, we experience a body shift; we feel freed up and relieved.
- Making space for and working through one feeling sometimes allow room for others to emerge.
- Reflecting on our experience of feeling our emotions through consolidates our gains and rewires our neural network.

CHAPTER 7

Step Four
Opening Up

And the day came when the risk to remain tight in a bud was more painful than the risk to bloom.

—Anaïs Nin

Nina let out a sigh of relief. Her biopsy results were negative. "Nothing to worry about," her doctor had said.

I can finally put this behind me, Nina thought to herself as she left the clinic. Without thinking she pulled out her cell phone to call her best friend, Maggie, but then stopped, suddenly feeling irritated. *She can call me,* she thought, and put her phone away.

The weekend prior to her appointment had been agonizing. Nina had tried to keep herself distracted, but couldn't stop worrying—playing out different scenarios in her head and feeling overwhelmed. But worse than her fear of possibly having cancer was the loneliness she'd felt. Her friends hadn't rallied around her as she had hoped. And although Nina was disappointed with them all, it was Maggie's absence that had hurt the most. Nina had thought that out of everyone, Maggie would have been there for her. After all, she'd have been right by Maggie's side had the roles been reversed. She always had. But ever since Nina found a lump in her breast, Maggie had become strangely distant. *I know it's probably scary for her as well,* Nina thought. *But what about me? I'm the one going through this.*

A few days passed before Maggie finally called, glad to hear that Nina was okay, wondering when they could get together. On the one hand, Nina was pleased to finally hear from her friend, but on the other, she still felt hurt. She wanted to cry, to share her sorrow with her friend, but she held back, afraid to show her true feelings and let Maggie back in.

A week later they met for lunch. Nina wondered if Maggie would say anything about her insensitivity around not calling sooner, maybe even apologize. But it never came up. Nina found herself feeling resentful as Maggie prattled on about this and that, and she almost said something to her, but got nervous and stopped herself, afraid of how Maggie might react. *Maybe now's not the time to go into this,* she reasoned, as she tried to push her feelings down inside.

But the pain behind her anger didn't go away. A wall formed around it, protecting Nina from feeling hurt . . . and keeping Maggie out.

A FAMILIAR KIND OF FEAR

Nina is afraid to let Maggie know how she feels. If she were able to be honest, to open up and share her feelings, maybe Maggie would understand and apologize. Maybe she'd get defensive or angry or hurt. Maybe the two of them would find a way to work through this difficult moment and heal the rupture in their friendship. At the very least, Nina might discover that she's able to deal with a challenging conversation, whatever the outcome. Instead, Nina keeps her feelings to herself and continues to feel resentful, hurt, and alone, and her relationship with Maggie continues to falter.

Reluctance to disclose our true feelings can hurt our relationships. Like Nina, we don't tell a loved one when we're hurt by something he or she did or didn't do. We stew in our anger or dismiss it, hoping it will disappear over time. We act strong or aloof, instead of admitting we're afraid. Or we get defensive—

blaming and criticizing, shutting down, pulling away—and hide what's really inside. We do whatever it takes to avoid exposing our vulnerability, afraid that we'll be met with criticism or rejection or will seem foolish and undesirable. Afraid we'll lose whatever connection we have.

Although fear of our own feelings is part of what keeps us from opening up to others, there's actually more to the story.

People come to me feeling frustrated and confused. They don't understand why it's so difficult for them to open up emotionally. They want to let others know how they feel, but they can't bring themselves to do it. It's too scary. Most of us think that this fear is specific to our current situation, but it actually originates in an early interpersonal context where the threat of reprimand or abandonment *was* a reality. Early experiences with our caregivers have led us to fear not only our emotions but also the consequences of expressing them. On some level, we're still afraid that sharing our feelings will threaten our relationships— so we hold them back, as Nina did. She's afraid to express her hurt and anger toward Maggie out of fear that Maggie might react negatively and that they'll lose their close connection with one another, so she says nothing.

But we don't have to live this way. Just as our fear of our feelings is based in old programming and can be changed, so too can our fear of how others will react. We just need to find a way to face our fear and be confident that we can deal with the consequences of expressing our feelings, partly because of having come to know and appreciate our feelings and their importance in our life, and partly because we know, through continued practice, that most people can handle our feelings and will ultimately appreciate our honesty.

Certainly, the people with whom we choose to share our feelings play a critical role in our experience. If they aren't ready or able to stay present or to receive and respond to our feelings in a constructive way, we're not going to get very far. Sometimes sharing our feelings only makes matters worse. (If you have concern that someone may be intolerant of your feelings and even hostile, then sharing your feelings isn't recommended, and you may want to seek assistance from a skilled therapist.) But too often we underestimate a friend's or loved one's capacity to be receptive and appreciative, and shy away from communicating our feelings altogether. We don't even try, and thus deny ourselves the possibility of something better. As the saying goes, nothing ventured, nothing gained.

I can't tell you how often clients of mine are surprised by how well it goes when they've taken the risk to open up with someone in their lives. They discover that they're able to stay present and see it through, and that it's not as scary as they had thought it would be. And, equally important, they discover that the other person is able to stay present and see it through as well. In short, they discover a new way of relating.

Of course, sometimes it doesn't go as smoothly as we'd like. After all, relationships are complex, and we can't control the outcome of every interaction. But we can learn to maximize the likelihood that our feelings will be heard and responded to positively. We can improve our ability to stay present and can learn and grow from the challenges we face. The first step is to be willing to open up and find out what's possible.

Part of what makes sharing our feelings such a scary prospect is that we're just not sure how to go about it. We don't know where to begin. We're unclear about what we want or need. We're not sure how best to communicate what's in our heart.

It's no wonder that we're confused and not sure what to do. Our avoidance has kept us from developing the skills needed to understand and effectively share our feelings. But we can learn. This chapter lays out a road map that you can use to help you navigate this new and different terrain. You'll also learn several useful skills that with regular practice will smooth out the road as you open up and share your feelings with others.

GETTING STARTED

The first step in communicating our feelings to others is understanding them ourselves. When we take the time to slow down and mindfully attune to our feelings, we discover their inherent wisdom—one of the many "resources" that become available to us when we're able to experience our emotions fully. If we listen closely to what our feelings are saying, it's surprising just how much they tell us. Like a wise sage, they

1. Impart information
2. Provide insight
3. Give us guidance

By connecting with and considering each of these aspects, we raise our self-awareness and deepen our self-understanding. Doing so also puts us in touch with our wants and needs. We're then in a much better place to make an informed choice about where we want to go next.

Let's take a closer look at the kinds of things we can learn when we pay attention to the wisdom of our feelings.

Information

Emotions let us know when things are right and when they're wrong, when life is going well and when it's not. When we're able to be fully present with and attuned to our feelings, the messages they convey are often simple and clear. Here are a few of the general themes:

- Anger informs us that we're being offended in some way.
- Love lets us know that someone or something is important to us, that we're connected and care deeply.
- Fear tells us that we're in danger.
- Happiness tells us that our needs are met and things are going well.
- Guilt lets us know that we're doing or have done something wrong.
- Shame signals to us that we're feeling overexposed and vulnerable.

Understanding the core messages of our feelings is an essential first step toward figuring out how we want to respond. This isn't a matter of thinking about feelings, but of connecting with them and what they're telling us. To do so requires that we spend some time listening to what our feelings are communicating. For instance, Nina's sadness signaled to her that something was off. As she tuned in to this feeling and wondered what it was telling her, it let her know how hurt she felt that her friends had backed away and that Maggie had all but disappeared. She then understood more clearly why she was feeling so upset.

You can use the Information Tool to help you get in touch with what your feelings are telling you.

Information Tool: What Are You Trying to Tell Me?

As you consider whether you want to share your feelings with others, spend some time listening to what they're saying to you.

1. Get quiet, go inside, and focus on your feelings.
2. Ask your feelings what they're trying to tell you. What are the messages they're communicating? What do they want you to know?
3. Give yourself some space and listen for the answer. Let it come from your feelings. If an answer doesn't come right away, let yourself stay open so that you'll be able to receive it when it does.

Insight

Once we understand the basic information our feelings are conveying, the next step is to become aware of whether there are underlying needs trying to be acknowledged as well. If we're angry, what do we need? If we're feeling happy, what do we want to do? If we're afraid, what would help us feel safe? Our emotions know what's best for us and can lead us to the answers to these questions. For instance, if Julie's father, whom we observed in Chapter Four when Julie called him to share her good news, reflected on his tepid response and was able to feel some guilt for not being more supportive of his daughter, perhaps he would recognize a desire to change his behavior or to make amends. In Chapter Six, we could see that Brian's anger was letting him know that he needed to be treated with respect and that he wanted his mother to respond accordingly. Similarly, Nina's sadness is telling her that she needs to let herself experience the pain of her friend's absence and that she wants Maggie to step forward, be empathic, and apologize for not being there for her.

If Nina were to let her guard down and acknowledge her needs and wants, she might open up and communicate them to Maggie and increase the likelihood of getting the support she longs for. But she doesn't. In addition to fearing how Maggie might react, Nina feels conflicted about her need for emotional support. She's not alone.

Many people view any kind of dependency as a sign of weakness. They think that as adults we should be emotionally self-sufficient and not need the support or reassurance of others (let alone admit that we do). Yet despite its popularity in western culture, this kind of thinking flies in the face of our contemporary understanding of human nature. As attachment theorist John Bowlby explained and ample research has confirmed, our needs for closeness, security, and care are biologically based, and they exist not just in childhood but throughout our lifetime.[1] Our ability to grow and flourish depends on having close, mutual connections with others. Being able to rely on and make use of others' emotional support—what could be referred to as "healthy dependency"—is a sign of strength and resilience, not weakness.

Although it may take courage to do so, admitting that we have emotional needs merely means that we're just like everybody else. We're human. We need to remind ourselves of this fact, and try to listen to the inclinations of our heart with a compassionate ear. After all, if we don't take our needs seriously, who will? And denying them only perpetuates our suffering. We end up feeling sad all the time, angry all the time, or constantly afraid. The feelings that our wants and needs generate keep coming back until we heed their call and do something to address them. Responding to our needs and wants may mean going against the grain of the societal messages we have absorbed, the lessons we learned in our families, or the critical voice we hear in our head, but it's the only way to get back to an authentic connection with ourselves and others.

You can use the Insight Tool to help you identify any underlying wants and needs you may be experiencing.

Guidance

Once we understand what our feelings are communicating, and identify and acknowledge our emotional needs or wants, we can

Insight Tool: What Do I Want or Need?

1. Put judgment aside, quiet your critical voice, and tune in to your feelings.
2. Ask yourself, *What do I want? What do I need? What are my heart's desires?* Let the answer come from your felt experience.
3. When you have a sense of what it is you'd like, try putting it into words and see if it rings true to you. If it doesn't, try again. You don't need to figure out what to do, or how to make it happen (we'll get to that in the next section); just acknowledge and accept what is. For example, had Nina listened to what her feelings were telling her and put her desires into words, she might have said, "I need Maggie to understand and appreciate how disappointed I was that she wasn't there for me. I would like her to apologize."

then figure out *if* and *how* we want to respond. At times, we might choose simply to be aware of our feelings and keep them to ourselves. Not all feelings need to be expressed to be of benefit to us. For instance, we might find ourselves feeling guilty for not spending more time with loved ones and then respond by making more of an effort to connect with them. Or we might feel happy about its being a beautiful day and be content just to savor the experience on our own.

At other times, our feelings move us to take action. In general, that's why they occur. As Daniel Goleman explains in his groundbreaking book *Emotional Intelligence*, "All emotions are, in essence, impulses to act, the instant plans for handling life that evolution has instilled in us."[2] They ready us to respond and, like a compass, point us in a direction that maximizes our ability to manage whatever comes our way. For example, anger readies us to defend ourselves, happiness prompts us to open up, and fear urges us to flee. Once we're aware of and able to experience our feelings, we then have a choice to make: whether to act on them or not.

Up until this point, our main focus has been on expanding the ability to experience and be present with our feelings. But we've come to a place in the process that requires a different aspect of emotional mindfulness. For us to make the best decision about whether or not to act on our feelings, we need to thoughtfully consider how we want to respond.

At times, we may choose simply to follow their prompt. For instance, sadness may be telling us that we need to take time to grieve, so we do just that. We slow down, turn inward, and give ourselves the space to mourn. But when it comes to sharing our feelings with others, there tend to be other factors that need to be considered. Asking yourself some questions can help you figure out how best to proceed. For instance:

- *What is my goal? What do I want to be different? What actions can I take that will make this happen?* Goals are often related to our needs and wants. For example, we might *want* to be closer to a loved one. Therefore, connecting more deeply would be our goal, and sharing our feelings would be a response that could help us achieve it.

- *Is there a problem? Will sharing my feelings help fix it?* For instance, as we saw in Chapter Six, Brian's mother's behavior was a problem. Letting her know that he finds it unacceptable and won't tolerate it any longer might improve the situation for him. But then again, if his mother is too closed off to hear him, it might not. Brian would need to consider what sort of response would be in his best interest and then decide how he wants to go about communicating with his mother.

- *How do I want to respond? What do I want to do? Will acting in this way be in keeping with my personal values?* For example, you might have the urge to tell someone off, but having a reasoned discussion might be more in line with a personal value of treating others with respect and integrity.

- *Is this the best time? the best setting? Should I wait until later?* Sometimes we need to wait until a more appropriate time or place to express our feelings. For instance, suppose that while at a social function, a friend or partner says something that's offensive. It would probably be better to wait until afterward to talk about it, when the matter can be dealt with in private.

- *Do I feel safe with this person? Do I trust him or her? Will he or she be respectful of my feelings?* Feeling safe about opening up is essential. We need to consider whether we can sufficiently trust the other person to risk opening up about our feelings. At the same time, emotional disclosure can build trust. Sometimes we need to take a chance and see how it goes.

Sometimes, when we're mindful of our feelings, it's easy to see the best course of action. As best-selling author Melody Beattie explains in her book *Choices: Taking Control of Your Life and Making It Matter,* when we let our feelings guide us, "It can be like magic. We just naturally know what to do next."[3] But at other times, we need to give ourselves room to pause, reflect, and figure out what we want to do. Fortunately, we have the collective wisdom of our feelings on our side to illuminate the way.

You can use the questions in this section to help you decide how you'd like to proceed. In addition, the Direction Tool combines the information we've covered thus far into a three-step process that you can also use as a guide.

Direction Tool

1. Get quiet, go inside, and ask your feelings what they are trying to tell you.
2. As you listen to your feelings, notice whether there are any underlying wants or needs trying to be realized.
3. Identify your goal and take some time to consider what course of action would best help you reach it.

HEEDING THE CALL

Some days after she'd last seen Nina, Maggie was shopping at her favorite store. Maggie loved to shop for a bargain. It was something that she and Nina would normally do together, but Nina was too busy to join her today. At least that's what she had said. Maggie maneuvered her way through the racks of clothes, glancing over things one last time to make sure she didn't miss anything good. Out of the corner of her eye, something caught her attention, and she turned to look. *That dress is so Nina,* she thought to herself. *She would love that!*

As she stopped to check it out, Maggie began to think about the phone conversation she had had with Nina earlier in the day. Maggie had tried to brush it off, but something about it had left her feeling unsettled. Nina had seemed distracted, not quite herself, maybe even a little annoyed. She'd said she was "busy" and "had things to do," but Maggie had sensed there was more going on. Something just hadn't seemed right. As a matter of fact, things hadn't felt right between the two of them for a few weeks. Concerned, Maggie traced back over time in her head, wondering if there was anything she had said or done that had upset Nina.

And then it dawned on her: *I wonder if she's mad at me for not calling her sooner when she had her biopsy. That must be it,* Maggie thought to herself and then started to feel angry. *She knew I had a lot going on then. Why is she making such a big deal over this? She worries about everything. She needs to get over herself!* Disgruntled, Maggie tried to put it out of her mind as she paid for her purchases and headed to the car.

The truth of the matter was that Maggie hadn't been too busy to call Nina. In fact, up until Nina had gotten her biopsy results, Maggie couldn't stop thinking about her, worrying that something might be seriously wrong. *What if Nina had cancer? How could I deal with that?* The whole thing just wigged her out.

Maggie went to put the key in the ignition, but stopped herself as her defensiveness softened. She sat for a moment staring out the window, and her thoughts went to Nina. *I'll bet she's feeling hurt,* Maggie thought to herself, as a sinking feeling came over her. She had tried to avoid feeling guilty about not being there for Nina whenever the thought had crept into her head, but she couldn't hold it back anymore. *I really dropped the ball this time.* She stayed with the feeling, wondering what she should do, and then something shifted. Maggie sat up straight. *This is ridiculous,* she thought as she started the car. *I need to talk to her.*

THE POWER OF WORDS

With this realization, Maggie is making good use of the wisdom of her feelings. Once she got past her initial frustration with Nina, she discovered that deep down inside, she actually felt guilty for not being there for her friend. She could admit that she'd "dropped the ball" and felt bad about doing so. Once she got in touch with her guilt, Maggie was inspired to make amends and repair the injury to the friendship. She set out to accomplish this goal by talking to Nina.

Letting someone know how we feel is the next step in the process of opening up. Although actions often speak louder than words, people can't really know for certain what's going on inside us—what we're feeling, what we may want or need—unless we tell them. And as psychologist Sue Johnson points out in her book *Hold Me Tight,* "The truth is, we will never create a really strong, secure connection if we do not allow our [loved ones] to know us fully."[4] Putting our feelings into words is one of the most powerful ways to communicate what's in our heart and to build emotionally close relationships.

In fact, sometimes the words can be what matter the most. An elderly client of mine recently shared with me that her husband of many years had never apologized in the entire history of their marriage. Although she sensed that he had been remorseful when he'd hurt her feelings, she also felt deprived of the kind of closeness that could have come had her husband been able to put his feelings into words, had he been able to say, "I'm sorry." At the same time, this woman was not able to let her husband know how she felt or to ask for what she needed from him. How sad that it was so hard for these two people to open up more deeply to each other even after all the time they'd been together.

Although this couple's experience may seem extreme, it's not uncommon. Many of us have a difficult time expressing our true feelings. We're not accustomed to speaking from a deeper, more core place inside us, nor are we sure what it entails. Somehow we think that expressing how we feel is just a matter of getting our feelings off our chest or out of our system. Opening up is something very different. Unlike venting, it is a guided verbal expression of what we feel inside and of our wants and needs. The main objective is to be able to express ourselves in a manner that is respectful of ourselves *and* of those to whom we open up.

EXPRESSING YOURSELF

The first step in the process of expressing yourself is to state how you feel. We've already discussed this earlier; in fact, the same guidelines you learned in Chapter Five for naming a feeling can be applied here as well. For example, when verbalizing emotional experience, it's best to keep it simple and stick to two- or three-word phrases ("I feel sad," "I'm feeling angry," "I'm afraid," and so on). A short statement can have strong impact and leaves little room for interpretation. You don't want someone unnecessarily confused after you've mustered the courage to open up. To that end, use words that refer to the basic emotions and avoid those that are vague or general, such as "good," "bad," or "upset." Vague words such as these make it difficult for the listener to connect with and clearly understand your emotional state. Likewise, steer clear of the ever popular trap of talking about what you *think* rather than what you *feel*. Remember, if you find yourself saying "like" or "that" after "I feel," you're probably expressing an opinion, judgment, or thought, rather than expressing feelings. It's okay to talk about what you think, but not when trying to express how you feel.

Next, acknowledge *why* you feel what you're feeling. This part usually has to do with either a life challenge (for example, a loved one's being ill, not getting a job you applied for, missing a close friend) or an interaction with someone (for example, a friend or loved one has said or done something that's led you to feel angry, sad, or threatened). In the latter situation, it's important to take responsibility for what you're feeling and refrain from blaming or criticizing the other person. Even though the person may have played a big role in eliciting the emotion, in the end they're y*our* feelings, no one else's.

Aim to communicate your feelings in a way that minimizes the chances that the other person will get defensive and increases the likelihood that he or she will be able to hear what you have to say. Speaking in the first person and using "I" statements helps us own the experience and personalize the communication. In addition, focusing the statement on the specific behavior that evoked the feelings rather than on the person himself or herself (for example, "I feel angry when you interrupt me," rather than

"You make me so angry") makes the message easier to receive. A good rule of thumb is to think about how you'd want to hear whatever you need to say if it were being expressed to you.

Then include a statement about what you want or need in order to make things better. Sometimes this part is implicit. For instance, you might simply be looking for an empathic shoulder to lean on, to be able to talk about your experience and get some support. At others times, the request may need to be more explicit. For instance, you may need to directly ask for comfort, for a boundary to be respected, or for recognition and validation. This piece can be challenging because it means admitting that you're vulnerable and have needs. But think of it this way: in general our friends and loved ones want to be helpful to us, but don't always know exactly what we need. How can they know unless we tell them? When we put our desires into words, we provide them with useful guidance and make it easier for them to respond. The guidelines we've discussed thus far apply here as well: be specific about what you need; keep it simple; use "I" statements ("I would like you to . . . ," "I want you to . . . ," "I would appreciate it if . . ."); and communicate in a respectful, nonblaming way.

To see the three steps in action, let's revisit Brian from Chapter Six as an example. If Brian were to let his mother know how he feels, he might say something like this: "Mom, my relationship with you is important to me. I don't want to become even more distant just to be polite. I'm feeling angry because of a comment you made. I'd appreciate it if you would be more sensitive to my feelings and treat me with respect." Brian starts off by letting his mother know that he values their relationship. He then states how he feels, explains why he's feeling that way, and asks for what he needs to improve the situation.

These steps in opening up are meant to be used as a guide; they're not hard-and-fast rules, nor do you have to start the process before you're ready. In the land of emotional communication, there's room for flexibility. Take the time you need, and work on it as you go. You might want to state your feelings out loud to yourself to hear how they sound and feel. You can practice getting used to them by writing them down until they seem right. The important thing is eventually to find a way to talk about your experience. You may make mistakes along the way, you may struggle to find the words, you may need to erase the blackboard and try again, but that's how you build and improve communication skills. That's how you learn to express yourself and find a way to connect.

MINDFUL COMMUNICATION

Even with a good deal of preparation, opening up to others may still feel scary. It brings us face-to-face with our fear that expressing our feelings will evoke a negative reaction and jeopardize the security of our relationships. But in the end, communicating our feelings is just what is needed to put our fear to rest. Fortunately, there are things we can do to take the edge off and make it easier to move forward. Although understanding that this fear is a remnant of the past can help diminish its intensity, practicing emotional mindfulness is what will really ease the way.

First and foremost, you need to stop and intentionally create the time and space to open up—otherwise it's just not going to happen. You'll keep rolling along right past precious opportunities to connect with others. Or you'll feel rushed and not give the process its due. You need to push the Pause button, disengage from the busyness of your life, and make some room to address, experience, and share your feelings. This doesn't need to be challenging. After all, it can happen at any time—on a walk, over dinner, while driving somewhere in the car. You can make a date to get together, or it can be more spontaneous. Almost any moment holds the potential for a deeper connection. You just need to set your mind to making it happen and then seize the moment before you.

Next, slow down and tune in to your experience using some of the ways you've learned already: concentrating on your breathing, mindfully observing your moment-to-moment experience, and simply reminding yourself to slow down.

Paying attention to what's going on in your body can help anchor you more fully in the present (for example, sensing your feet on the ground, your seat in the chair; noticing any and all bodily sensations). Once grounded, pay attention to other aspects of your experience as well. Shift your attention from noticing what's happening inside you to how the other person is responding and to what's transpiring between the two of you. Repeatedly returning your attention to what's going on will help you feel more grounded in the here and now and, as a result, feel less inhibited by fear.

Speaking slowly and more deliberately is calming and can help deepen your connection to yourself. When we're excited or feeling anxious, it's common to talk rapidly. I know I certainly do. When this happens, as is true of any time we hurry, it's harder to hold on to our emotional center. It also raises our anxiety. Slowing down the rate at which we speak gives us more space to feel and reflect mindfully on what we're saying and, in doing so, allows our expression to truly come from the heart. It's simple enough to do, yet it can yield powerful results.

Making eye contact also brings us more directly into the present moment, although it can sometimes feel threatening. We're afraid of what we'll see in the other person's face, so we look away. When we do this, we miss an opportunity to confront and possibly disprove our fear. So often in my work with couples, when they find the courage to look into each other's eyes, they're surprised to see the opposite of what they were expecting. Instead of disdain, they see empathy. Instead of anger, they see vulnerability. Instead of fear, they see compassion. When they really make an effort to take in the other person, the present reality comes into clearer focus, and their past fears begin to fade. They begin to see that sharing their feelings doesn't have to be frightening. It's a little like turning on the light in the closet for a child to show him or her that there aren't any monsters there to be afraid of. Of course, a lot depends on who it is that we choose to open up to. But at the very least, even if the other person appears to be uncomfortable or anxious, we learn that we can handle their discomfort and that it's not something to be afraid of.

Making eye contact has other benefits. It makes us feel closer to the other person and helps us get emotionally "in sync." When we witness someone crying, laughing, or getting angry, on some level we share the experience. We feel what the other person is feeling as well. Although we've long understood emotions to be contagious, recent research by neuroscientist Giacomo Rizzolatti and his colleagues at the University of Parma in Italy has identified the brain mechanisms underlying this phenomenon. The researchers discovered that when we observe another person's emotions or actions, nerve cells in our brain dubbed "mirror neurons" fire as though we're doing or experiencing the same thing.[5] For instance, when we see someone in distress, the "distress area" in our own brain is also activated, and we feel it as well. When we make eye contact, when we open up and let others see our feelings, it increases the likelihood that they'll be able to understand and empathize with our experience (and vice versa).

The first step can be the hardest. But at some point, despite any discomfort we might feel, we just need to go for it. As bestselling author Susan Jeffers suggests, we need to "feel the fear and do it anyway."[6] You can use the Mindful Communication Tips to guide you as you move forward.

Mindful Communication Tips

When opening up and sharing your feelings, practice the following:

- Feel yourself grounded in your body. Notice your feet against the floor, your seat against the chair. Bring your attention back to this place when you start to feel anxious.
- Speak slowly and allow yourself to stay connected to your words. Pause and reflect on what you're saying and try to feel the words coming from a centered place inside you.
- Without judgment, observe what's happening in the moment, what's coming up for you, what's transpiring between you and the other person, how the other person is responding. Just notice.
- Let yourself make eye contact. Notice what you see in the other person's eyes. If you're not sure what he or she is feeling, ask for clarification.

NOT SO HARD AFTER ALL

Nina found an empty table near the back of the coffee shop and took a seat facing the door so that she could see when Maggie arrived. She took a sip of tea and tried to relax. At first, Nina was relieved to get Maggie's message suggesting they get together "and talk." But now, as the moment approached, she felt anxious. She had wanted to talk to Maggie for a while, to let her know how disappointed she'd felt, but she had kept putting it off.

Nina looked up and saw Maggie heading toward her. Her heart sped up. She took a deep breath and tried to calm herself. *Here we go,* she thought to herself.

It wasn't long before the initial small talk began to wane. Suddenly they found themselves sitting face-to-face in silence. It was Maggie who gently started the ball rolling. "So . . . I've been wondering if there's something going on?" she said. "I mean, I don't know how *you* feel, but things just haven't felt right between us."

"Yeah . . . I know. They haven't," Nina admitted, a bit tentative at first. "I . . . I've wanted to say something to you but, I don't know, the longer I didn't, the harder it got for me to bring it up. And you know how I can just . . . ," Nina almost erupted into a flurry of words, the emotion of the moment about to get away from her, but she stopped herself and tried to slow down. She sat very still and then looked at Maggie. Her eyes filled up with tears as emotion began to surface. She took a breath and said, "Um, I was really hurt when I had my biopsy and you weren't there. I mean, you're my best friend and . . ." Her voice began to break. She looked down, her sadness breaking through, and began to cry.

Maggie extended her hand and touched Nina's arm. "I'm really sorry," she said.

Nina looked up, and their eyes met. Maggie looked pained. She had tears in her eyes as well.

"I don't know what to say." Maggie continued, "I really don't have a good excuse. I guess it kind of freaked me out. I mean . . . what would I do if something happened to you?"

"I know. I figured that. But it scared me too. I really needed you then." Nina looked at Maggie's face and saw the regret in her eyes. The hurt and anger she felt inside began to fade. "I've really missed you," she said.

"I've missed you too."

SOMETHING BETTER

Opening up may be difficult at first, but you don't have to do it all at once. You can start small and work up to expressing yourself a little more each time. You can begin by simply acknowledging that you feel vulnerable. You can say, "This feels awkward for me. I'm not used to talking in this way," and then go from there.

The key to making progress is to try to lean into your discomfort a little more each time. When you start to feel more comfortable, take another step forward. See if you can stretch the moment when you're making eye contact, sitting in silence, listening to what the other is saying, staying with your feelings or the other's feelings. Encourage yourself to be with the experience a little longer each time. Over time, your capacity to open up and be emotionally present will expand.

At times, communicating your feelings may feel challenging, especially when difficult emotions come up. When the going gets tough, you can rely on your mindfulness skills to help you stay the course. When you're tempted to pull back or withdraw, keep bringing your attention back to the present moment. Take a moment to notice what's happening in your body, what's happening for the other person, what's happening between you. Keep grounding yourself in the here and now. Conflict is inevitable, so it's important to work through it. Trust and closeness grow over time as we reveal our true self and see that we can maintain our connection, even when doing so is difficult.

Opening up and sharing our feelings is a lifelong process. Practice making this way of communicating commonplace. The more you do it, the better you'll get, and the easier it will become.

When we share our feelings with others, we maximize our chances of working through a problem. We open the door to closer, stronger connections in which anger can be resolved, sadness and fear can be soothed, and love can be shared more deeply. When we express what's in our heart, we honor ourselves and our loved ones. We create the kinds of relationships we really want.

CHAPTER TAKE-HOME POINTS

- Our needs for closeness, security, and care are biologically based and exist throughout our lifetime.
- Emotions can help us see what we need or want in order to make things better.
- Putting our feelings into words is one of the most powerful ways to communicate what's in our heart.
- Early experiences with our caregivers can lead us to be afraid of opening up later in life.
- Fear of expressing ourselves can be overcome through practice and experience.
- When we are mindful of it, the wisdom of our feelings can inform and guide our choices.
- When verbalizing how we feel and what we need, we should keep our message simple and clear, use "I" statements, and communicate in a way that is respectful to ourselves and the listener.
- Slowing ourselves down and mindfully attending to the present moment can make opening up more manageable.
- Speaking slowly connects us to our feelings and allows our expression to come from the heart.
- Making eye contact helps extinguish our fears, makes us feel closer, and increases the likelihood of being understood.
- Lean into your discomfort a little more each time, and your capacity to be emotionally open will expand.

CHAPTER 8

Putting It All Together

In the midst of winter, I finally learned that there was in me an invincible summer.

—ALBERT CAMUS

TO THIS POINT, WE'VE EXPLORED EACH OF THE FOUR STEPS to overcoming feelings phobia. Now comes the time to put them all together. In this chapter, we revisit several of the people you've met earlier and take a look at how they worked with the four steps and the skills we've discussed and made use of them in their lives.

ALEX: THE GIFT OF GRIEF

Alex stepped back to get a good look at the Christmas tree and noticed a bare spot that needed a decoration or two. He surveyed the clutter of boxes on the floor and saw one with the lid still on. *I knew there had to be a few more left,* he thought to himself as he picked up the box and sat down on the couch to look them over. As he removed the lid, he immediately recognized the ornaments he and his wife had found on their vacation in Maine a few summers ago. He was about to call out to her in the other room when something else caught his attention. It was the ceramic snowman he had made in school as a child. He remembered the day he gave it to his parents, so proud of his creation. His mother had made a big fuss. Every year thereafter, she would comment as she hung it on the tree that it was her favorite decoration of all. She was always so sweet that way.

Alex's heart ached. Although it had been a few years since his parents' tragic death, holidays continued to be emotionally challenging for him. It seemed that he missed them most of all this time of year. His throat tightened as the tears welled up inside him, and he felt the urge to get up and busy himself as his wife entered the room. It had been difficult for him to be vulnerable in front of her, but he was tired of holding back and wanted to be closer. Alex looked down at the ornament for a moment and took a deep breath, trying to settle his nerves a bit, then looked at his wife.

"What's the matter, Al? Are you okay?" she asked, concerned by the pain she saw in his face.

"Um, it's my parents. I was just thinking about them," he admitted, and then looked back down. She sat next to him and put her arm around him. Alex was about to tell her about the ornament, but stopped himself. His wife's presence was comforting, and he felt as though he could melt. He could feel the sadness inside him rising up, and instead of pushing it back down as he'd done so many times in the past, he tried something different. He shifted his weight slightly to feel more grounded on the couch and then took a deep breath. *Just let it come,* he told himself and slowly exhaled as he gave way to his feelings. The sadness in him broke through, and tears came streaming down his cheeks. His wife rubbed his back as he cried deeply.

Afterward, the two of them sat together quietly, holding hands. Alex thought about what had just happened, about how he had let his guard down and opened up to his wife. About how he had cried so hard and now actually felt better for it. The grief he felt only a few moments ago had passed, and in its wake was a sense of relief. He thought about his parents, and now, instead of sadness, he felt a sense of warmth and connection.

Alex looked at his wife. He felt so close to her in that moment. His eyes filled with tears. But this time they were different. These were tears of gratitude, not sadness. His heart swelled as he squeezed his wife's hand and said tenderly, "You know, I really love you."

She smiled with deep affection and said, "I love you too."

❋

Alex's experience is fairly straightforward. He was aware of his sadness as well as the urge to avoid it, and instead of holding back, he grounded himself, took a deep breath, and gave way to his feelings. When he then reflected on his experience, he discovered that feeling his way through his grief had brought him to a positive place where he felt more connected to his wife as well as to his parents. Where once there was pain, his heart was now filled with love and gratitude. He is changing his relationship with his emotions as well as the associations in his brain.

We often worry that giving way to sadness will make matters worse, that we'll miss whatever we've lost even more. But actually the opposite is true. Grief, particularly when it's shared, leads to comfort and healing, sometimes even happiness. It clears away the dark clouds of pain and sadness so that we're able to see and more readily connect with the warm loving feelings and memories that are also there inside us.

LAUREN: BEFRIENDING FEAR

Lauren put down her book. She had thought she might be able to get some reading done, but she couldn't stop thinking about the conversation she had yesterday with her boyfriend, Nick. Now and then, Nick would make comments that led her to believe that he was planning on marrying her, but whenever Lauren tried to talk about the subject more directly, he would become evasive or withdraw. This recent conversation seemed to go a little better. Or had it? Now she wasn't so sure. As she replayed it in her head, she realized that although Nick's tone seemed reassuring at the time, he hadn't really answered any of her questions about their future together.

Lauren began to feel unsettled.

I know he's afraid, she thought to herself. His parents had a rocky marriage, and that scares him. He's probably worried that we could end up the same way. Maybe I'm just being impatient. Maybe I just need to give him a little more time and he'll come around. Maybe I . . . Lauren caught herself. She recognized that she was once again making excuses and about to get lost in her thoughts instead of listening to her feelings. The truth was that no matter how hard she tried, Nick hadn't "come around" in the two years they'd been together. And it wasn't just in their relationship that he was struggling. He was stuck in a job he didn't like, had stopped communicating with his family, and was letting his health go. Lately, Lauren had been encouraging him to see a therapist to address whatever issues were making it hard for him to move forward, but he couldn't seem to take action.

Lauren sat up, feeling motivated to try to be with her herself in a deeper way. She shifted her focus away from the chatter in her head and tried to tune in to what was going on inside her. At first she didn't notice anything. But as she paid attention to her body, she became aware of a bit of constriction in her chest. As she focused in on it and tried to stay present with her experience, she also noticed that her heart was beating fast and that she felt kind of shaky. Lauren shifted her attention to a pleasant image to try to calm herself. She pictured herself at the lake, standing on the dock, listening to the lapping of the water and smelling the fresh air. She stayed with the experience a moment and then refocused on what she was feeling in her body.

As she tuned in to her internal experience, she realized that deep down she was feeling afraid. She was scared that Nick would never change. That even if they did get married, he'd never actually deal with his problems. How could she depend on him to take care of a family if he wasn't willing to take care of himself?

Lauren began to cry as the pain of her dawning awareness came over her. She loved Nick, but it didn't seem to be enough. If he wasn't going to do the work to get unstuck, and so far he hadn't, they'd never have the kind of relationship she wanted for herself. It took courage to face her feelings, to listen to what they were telling her. And it hurt. There was so much about Nick that she loved, that she would miss if this didn't work out.

Although it pained her to think about ending their relationship and starting over, she felt some sense of clarity for the first time in a long time. She wanted something more for herself. She wasn't sure that she could find it with Nick, or anyone else for that matter, but she also wasn't willing or ready to sacrifice her dream of something better. She knew that she needed to honor what her fear was telling her: that ultimately she wanted and needed something more out of a relationship in order to be truly happy.

As Lauren wiped away her tears, she felt resolved to tell Nick how she felt, see how he responded, and then figure out where to go from there.

❉

By recognizing her tendency to get lost in her thoughts and then shifting her focus to her body, and by using visualization to calm herself and then refocusing on her internal experience, Lauren was able to identify, face, and begin to make use of her core feeling of fear. In the process, she was learning that moving toward her fear, instead of away from it, is hugely beneficial.

Fear can be a challenging emotion to slow down for, to stay present with, especially because it makes us want to run. But our fear is often telling us there's something important that we need to pay attention to. Sometimes we mistakenly try to dismiss fear. We tell ourselves we're overreacting, or minimize its severity and say that it's "no big deal," we can handle it. When we do that, we may miss an important message.

Although it's essential that we incorporate rational thinking into our assessment process and evaluate whether our fear is relevant to the here and now—after all, we know how that old amygdala of ours can sometimes be off the mark—we need to first listen to what our fear is telling us. As Lauren discovered, when she was able to attend to her fear, it was giving her vital information about her relationship, about her choice in a life partner. And if she can stay attuned to her feelings, she can use them as a guide as she tries to decide what to do.

JULIE: MAKING ROOM FOR JOY

Julie's boss pulled her aside as they left the meeting. "I just want to tell you how impressed I am with how you handled this project," he said. "We wouldn't have gotten this account if it wasn't for you."

"Well, I give the team a lot of credit," she responded, feeling a little uncomfortable with the compliment. "We all worked hard to make it happen."

"I'm aware of that, but it was under your leadership. You're the one who pulled this all together. You're quite an asset to this department. I'm very glad you're here."

"Well, thanks," she said with a smile. "I'm glad I'm here, too."

Julie contained herself as she quickly walked back to her office, shut the door, and then, when no one could see her, broke into a little victory dance. She'd been working on this pitch for weeks, and it couldn't have gone better. Julie felt a rush of energy and then, suddenly feeling uncomfortable again, pulled herself back. *Okay, okay, she thought, let's not get out of control. There's still a lot more work to do.* She straightened her jacket, sat down at her desk, and tried to focus on her work.

That evening, as Julie rode the train home, she thought about the events of the day. She felt a sense of happiness flutter through her and then shifted her attention and started rifling through her bag. *Wait a minute,* she thought to herself as she noticed what she was doing. *This is a big deal. I need to let myself really take it in.* She put down her bag, closed her eyes, and encouraged herself to spend a little more time with her positive feelings. She called to mind the interaction she had with her boss. She remembered him say, *You're quite an asset to this department. I'm very glad you're here.* Julie smiled as she felt a warm tingling sensation start to radiate through her upper body like the rays of the morning sun beginning to brighten a room.

And then, seemingly out of nowhere, she felt a twinge of sadness. *That's weird,* Julie thought, slightly taken aback. *Why should I feel sad?* She was tempted to ignore it, but instead, Julie slowed herself down and tried to stay open. As she focused inward, her sadness grew; as she stayed with it, it took her back in time to a painful place. She saw herself much younger, feeling disappointed and hurt. Her father, a chronic alcoholic, never acknowledged her achievements. For years, Julie had tried to get his attention by doing anything she could to inspire even an inkling of pride in him, but was always left feeling as though she wasn't good enough. As she got older, she struggled to put the pain of his neglect behind her, but, unattended to, it lingered inside and threatened to rear its head whenever something positive happened for her. Perhaps that's why she had such a hard time letting herself truly enjoy her accomplishments. How could she really celebrate her success with the pain of her father's lack of acknowledgment lurking in the background? Julie looked out the window and cried softly as she rode out a wave of sorrow. It wasn't a pleasurable experience. No—in fact, it hurt. But it also felt true and right.

By the time Julie reached her stop, something inside her had shifted. Although surely there were more feelings there regarding her experience with her father, in the moment she felt lighter, calmer. She thought about what had come up for her and how it made so much sense. It wasn't happiness that made her uncomfortable; it was all the unresolved pain and disappointment below the surface that would get triggered whenever she was positively acknowledged by others. Julie felt a sense of compassion toward herself as she understood more clearly why allowing herself to enjoy her successes had been such a struggle for her.

The next day, as Julie rode the train to work, she thought about how well the pitch had gone the day before. She saw herself sailing through the presentation and remembered breaking into a little victory dance in her office afterward. The memory made her smile. A warm, tingly sensation spread from her heart to all the corners of her being. She sat with it a while as it lingered inside her longer than usual.

❋

At first, Julie didn't realize she hadn't been allowing herself to fully experience her happiness. She wasn't aware of what was behind her minimizing her boss's compliments or short-circuiting her excitement. But when she later caught herself and made some room for her feelings, she discovered that by staying open and allowing her sadness to come forward, she could find out what had been getting in her way. And she could begin to heal the pain that had kept her from a happier existence.

Julie's difficulty with taking in praise and feeling proud of her achievements is very common. Although this kind of difficulty may just be about allowing ourselves to feel our feelings, sometimes, as it was for Julie, it may also reveal unresolved issues from the past, issues that need attention and care. Unfinished emotional business from the past can be challenging to work through. You may be able to feel your way through it on your own, but you may also find that you feel stuck. At times, it may be helpful to seek the help of a trained professional. To that end, I've included an appendix at the end of the book with information about therapy and coaching should you be interested in seeking further assistance.

BRIAN: UNCOVERING THE ROAD TO REPAIR

"There's one!" Brian said to his partner, Eric, as they circled the parking lot trying to find an open spot. It was ten minutes before the performance was to begin, and they still needed to pick up their tickets. Eric stepped on the gas, surging forward to grab the space, and almost collided with another car coming around the corner. He slammed on the brakes and then, somewhat out of character, laid on the horn. Brian could see the other driver looking incensed, and he yelled at Eric, "Quit honking the horn!" And then, rather harshly, "What's the matter with you? Do you want to get us beaten up by some idiot?"

As they hurried to the theater, Brian could tell that Eric was upset with him. "I'm sorry I lost it," Brian said, trying to make amends as they walked into the lobby. "That just freaked me out."

But Eric wasn't appeased. "Yeah, well, you've been pretty critical of me lately, and I'm getting kind of sick of it. Keep your comments to yourself," he said as he handed Brian a ticket and disappeared into the theater.

Brian stood there startled as Eric's words rang in his ears and then he thought, *Screw you. I tried to apologize,* and angrily made his way to his seat.

Brian tried to concentrate on the performance, but couldn't stop thinking about what had just happened. He kept playing the incident over and over in his head and felt angry whenever he thought about how Eric had responded to his apology. *He's so damn sensitive,* Brian thought to himself. *How did he expect me to react anyway? I mean, what the hell was he thinking when he honked at that guy? If he wants to be a big baby about it, fine. Let him.*

The two of them, both still irritated, barely talked to each other during the intermission.

At some point during the second act, Brian began to soften as he sensed that his anger might possibly be defensive. He was getting better at recognizing his tendency to dig in his heels and retreat to a distant internal place, to hold back on his more vulnerable feelings. Brian decided to try to stay open and look beyond his anger to see what else might be there. He thought about what Eric had said about his being critical lately and began to wonder if it might be true.

In reality, the last few weeks at work had been unusually stressful, and Brian hadn't exactly been the most fun to be around. In fact, he'd been pretty difficult. He wasn't the best when it came to dealing with stress. As he took a more honest look at himself, he recalled another incident in which he'd given Eric a hard time. Brian got a sick feeling in his stomach as a wave of shame came over him. *I'm such an idiot,* he thought, and could feel himself about to get sucked into a black hole of self-criticism and despair— an old way of responding. He took a deep breath and shifted in his seat so that he could feel more grounded in the present moment. The shame he was feeling got more intense for a moment, but then began to dissipate. A different feeling came to the fore. *I'm not an idiot,* Brian thought to himself, *but I've really been acting like one.* He closed his eyes as a feeling of guilt moved through him, and he tried to ride it out to the other side. He felt terrible about how he'd behaved toward Eric, this man he loved so dearly, and wanted to make amends. He knew what he needed to do.

In the car on the way home, Brian found the courage to open up. "Can we talk?" he asked.

"Sure," Eric replied, with a slight edge.

"Um, I've been thinking about what you said . . . about how I've been kind of critical of you lately." Brian felt a catch in his throat, took a deep breath, and continued. "You're right. I've been acting like a jerk. Work has been stressing me out and . . . well . . . I'm sure you've gotten the worst of me. I feel horrible about that and . . . I'm really sorry."

Eric looked over at Brian. He could see the regret in his eyes. He sighed and then said, "Thanks; that means a lot to me."

As he lay in bed that night, Brian thought about the evening. He felt good about how he was starting to do things differently. In the past, he would have gotten stuck in being argumentative, acting as though he didn't care, or shutting down. But this time he was able to recognize what was going on for him and try something new. And although it was hard to face the guilt he felt for how he'd been acting toward Eric, he could see how staying open to his feelings enabled him to move through them and, ultimately, make amends. Brian looked over at Eric, fast asleep beside him; he put his arm around him and pulled him close.

❄

It took Brian a little while to recognize that his angry response toward Eric's assertion was defensive. When he eventually let down his guard, his underlying feelings began to flow. Fortunately, Brian was aware of the difference between guilt and shame and could stop himself from getting caught up in the latter. Remember, guilt is about a behavior; shame is about the self. When he was able to identify, accept, and feel his way through his guilt, he became motivated to make amends.

Sometimes that's how things go. We get triggered and respond reflexively without realizing we're being defensive. That's when practicing emotional mindfulness is essential. If we're able to be present with our experience, to be mindful of it and stay open and curious to all that's there, we can get past a defensive response to connect with our core feelings. The more we relate to our inner experience in this way, the easier it becomes to see our way through to a better place.

KATE: GROWING INTO HAPPINESS

As she neared the end of her hike, Kate wondered about what had happened earlier. She had stopped to enjoy the view with her friends and, for some strange reason, started to feel anxious. *This is so like me,* Kate thought to herself. *I've been working my butt off for so long, and now, when I have a chance to relax and enjoy myself, I can't.* She was about to get down on herself, but, knowing how that would only make her feel worse, decided instead to get curious.

Later that day, while sitting by the pool, Kate thought about what had happened on her morning hike. As she replayed the experience in her head, she noticed that her chest began to tighten; she tried to stay with the uneasiness and see what it was about. As she focused inward, Kate noticed that her feet were tingling as well and that it felt hard to remain still. She put her hand on her heart and breathed deeply, trying to calm herself. As her anxiety began to loosen up, she became aware of a queasy feeling in her stomach. *What's that about?* she wondered. *Am I getting sick? Was it something I ate?* She thought about the restaurant she'd gone to with her friends the night before, the conversation they had over dinner, and then realized that her mind was wandering. Kate brought her attention back to the uncomfortable feeling in her stomach and tried to stay with it. At first she thought that it might be shame, but, inspecting it further, she realized that this experience felt different. Then it hit her: *I'm feeling guilty.*

Guilty? Why should I feel guilty? Kate wondered. She scanned back over the last few days to see if there was something she'd done wrong, but nothing stood out. As she focused back on the feeling, she got the sense that it was old, as though it came from a distant place. As she stayed with it, she let her mind drift back in time to see what she could learn. Kate saw herself as a little girl. Her mother had a crippling illness and was often in a great deal of physical pain. Kate remembered a time when she and her brother were playing and got a little carried away, as children often do. Her mother, who must have been having a particularly bad day, got upset and admonished them for adding to her distress. Over time, Kate ended up worrying that if she had a good time, if she let loose and really enjoyed herself, it would somehow make matters worse for her mother. And when she did start to enjoy herself, she felt guilty, as though she had done something wrong.

Kate realized that the anxiety and guilt she was feeling now was a holdover from the past. She felt compassion toward this younger part of herself that was still worried about the possible consequences of being exuberant and joyful. *I don't have to be afraid of letting go and enjoying myself anymore,* Kate told herself, and felt determined to turn things around.

That night, while out with her friends, Kate noticed a bit of the old anxiety fluttering in the background. This time she knew where it came from and didn't feel thrown as she had in the past. Instead, she reminded herself that she was entitled to have a good time and then made a conscious effort to embrace her positive feelings more fully and really enjoy herself. It turned out to be the best night of her vacation.

❇

Kate used emotional mindfulness to great effect. She recognized that she was avoiding her anxiety and then later focused in on it with curiosity. As she did, she became aware of different bodily sensations and attended to them. She calmed herself when her anxiety increased and stayed tuned in to what was going on inside her. When her attention drifted, she simply brought it back to her physical experience and tried to stay with it.

By allowing her guilt to come to the fore, by staying open to it and following it back in time, she uncovered the roots of her discomfort. Realizing that it came from an old place helped put things into a new perspective and made it easier to try something different.

The more Kate leans into her happiness, the more she breaks its old ties to anxiety, worry, and guilt. She's changing her relationship with her emotional experience and making it possible for her to experience her happiness more fully. And all the while she's going through this process, she's establishing new neural networks in her brain, which will expand her range of emotional options.

MARK: WAKING UP TO ANGER

Mark listened to the message from his brother with disbelief. "Hey, guy. Listen, it doesn't look like I'm going to be able to make it this weekend. Got an invite to go out on a buddy's boat that's too good to turn down. Sorry 'bout that, but, well . . . you know how it goes. Talk to you soon."

"No, I don't know how it goes," Mark said out loud as he pressed the delete button. *I'd never cancel on someone at the last minute,* he thought to himself. He'd been counting on his brother to help him paint his new place, and now he'd have to do it all himself. Somewhere inside him, Mark began to feel angry, but then that changed to a sinking feeling that seemed to drain the energy out of his body; he began to feel depressed.

Mark had been looking forward to spending some time with his brother. He'd imagined the two of them talking and maybe getting to know each other a little better as they worked on the house. After all these years, Mark still harbored the hope that he might have a different kind of relationship with his only brother. *I guess I just don't matter very much to him,* he thought to himself. *I mean, if I did, he'd be here. What's wrong with me?* Mark felt foolish for allowing himself even to imagine that things might be different, and proceeded to get down on himself.

The next morning, Mark dragged himself around the house as he tried to get started. He'd assumed that he'd be ready to go after a good night sleep, but instead he felt sluggish. *Why am I so tired?* Mark wondered, as he sat down on the floor and began to stir a can of paint. He ran through the last few days in his head trying to figure out what was up for him. It had been a busy week at work, but nothing out of the ordinary. But then he thought about getting his brother's message and realized that it was probably around then that his mood had changed. *So am I just feeling let down?* he asked himself. Disappointment was certainly a part of Mark's experience, but it felt as though there were more to it. Mark focused inward to try to get a clearer sense of what was going on for him emotionally. His body felt weighed down, and he noticed a heavy sensation in his chest that had a stale, lifeless quality to it. *What's that about?* he wondered. He sat with the question for a moment and then it occurred to him that underneath this malaise he might actually be feeling angry. As he considered this possibility, something inside him seemed to loosen up. Just then, Mark noticed a flash of irritation in his chest.

That's it! Mark thought. *Of course I feel angry.* And then, *This is what I do. I turn it on myself.* Increasingly, Mark was becoming aware of how he tended to defend against his anger. Without even knowing he was doing it, he'd take the anger out on himself and end up feeling miserable. *This has got to stop,* Mark thought to himself as he got up and started to roll some paint on the wall. He thought about his brother bailing on him, and as he did, his anger grew stronger. *That's so like him. He's so self-centered! And I keep letting him get away with it. Well, not anymore.* The energy flowed back into Mark's body, and he felt empowered. He wanted to call his brother right then and there and tell him off, but stopped himself, thinking it best to wait until he wasn't as worked up. He knew that he needed to stand up for himself and let his brother know how he felt.

A few days later, after giving some thought to what he wanted to say, Mark called his brother. They'd barely exchanged hellos before his brother launched into a monologue about how great his day of sailing was. Mark felt the anger stir inside him again and concentrated on his breathing to keep himself grounded as he waited for the opportunity to speak. Finally, his brother stopped and asked, "Hey, how'd you make out with your painting?"

"Fine, but, well, you know . . ." Mark slowed himself down. He wanted to be clear and to speak from a centered place. "I need to tell you that I was pretty disappointed and angry about your decision. I was counting on you to help me. And I was also really looking forward to doing something together."

"What?" his brother said, taken aback. And then, defensively, "Are you telling me you wouldn't have done the same thing?"

"That's not what I'm saying," Mark said, aware of his brother's tone. "But no, actually, I wouldn't have."

"Yeah right," his brother said, annoyed. And then, "Look, I can't help it if you didn't have someone else lined up. That's not my responsibility. You should have . . ."

He's trying to put this off on me, Mark thought to himself as his brother went on. *This is what he does. He blames everybody else.* Mark felt the urge to become argumentative, but stopped himself. He didn't want to get caught up in a defensive dance. He focused on his breathing again for a moment to calm himself and stay centered, and then said, "I'm not saying it was your responsibility to help me. What I'm trying to tell you is how it felt when you backed out."

"Give me a break. You're totally overreacting."

"Look, you don't have to agree with me. But I'd appreciate it if you could try to understand how it felt on this end. I was really disappointed, and it made me angry."

"Bud, you know, we can get together anytime."

Mark could tell that he wasn't getting very far. "You're not hearing what I'm saying, are you?"

"I'm hearing you fine. It just sounds like a lot of bull."

"I'm sorry you feel that way," Mark said. "It doesn't feel that way to me."

"Yeah . . . well . . . look, I should get going. I've got a lot to do."

Mark hung up the phone feeling dismayed, and wondered about how realistic his hope for a closer relationship with his brother might actually be.

✳

It was Freud who first suggested that depression is anger turned inward.[1] Although we now know that there are multiple causes for depression (for example, biological, genetic, and environmental), when a person suppresses anger, it certainly can affect his or her energy level and overall mood. Mark's defensive response to his anger is common. Instead of feeling angry toward the person who wronged us, we unconsciously turn it inward and end up feeling bad about ourselves. Despite the personal suffering that ensues, on some level this response feels safer. We're just not used to experiencing our anger in a healthy way or using it to confront the powerful people in our life. Fortunately, Mark was able to recognize his habitual response to his anger and turn it around.

But, as is sometimes the case, Mark's attempt to communicate with his brother and let him know how he felt didn't go so well. Although Mark handled himself admirably and made good use of his mindfulness skills to avoid getting pulled into a fight, his brother was unable to engage in a constructive manner. As we become more comfortable with our feelings, with honoring and expressing them, we sometimes discover that the people in our life have limitations. At times such as these, it can be helpful to practice empathy. After all, we have some personal understanding of what it's like to be afraid of one's feelings. Sometimes, by moving slowly and taking it one small step at a time, we can help our relationships stretch and grow emotionally. Sometimes we may choose simply to accept people for where they are and still enjoy a meaningful relationship. At other times, we may choose to reevaluate our hopes for the relationship and put our energy where we know it will be productive and yield the kind of relationships we really want to have. The important thing is that we not avoid opportunities to connect and communicate our feelings in our relationships with others. If the other person isn't able to accept our feelings, we can then decide where to go from there.

FRANK: FINDING THE COURAGE TO LOVE

Frank walked into the locker room and sat down on a bench. He'd just run into a buddy of his, who told him that a mutual friend of theirs was getting a divorce. Frank was surprised. He had no idea that Jeremy was having marital problems. *I know how that one goes,* he thought to himself. It had been a couple years since Frank's difficult divorce, and he was glad to have that mess well behind him. *I hope he has an easier time with it than I did,* Frank thought to himself, and began to change into his gym clothes.

As Frank made his way through his workout, he thought about how much better his life was now. Certainly his relationship with Rachel had a lot to do with that. They'd met about a year ago and started dating shortly thereafter. At first, Frank felt apprehensive about getting involved with anyone, but over time had grown more comfortable with being in a relationship again. How could he not? Rachel was so different from his ex-wife. She was really easy to be with and very thoughtful and caring. Today, for example, she called him for no particular reason other than to say, "I love you." Frank got a warm feeling inside and smiled as he thought about Rachel. He felt so lucky.

But as Frank continued along with his workout, he began to feel uneasy. Rachel was so generous with her loving feelings toward him, and he wasn't as demonstrative. He knew how much it meant to him to hear Rachel's reassuring words and, for a moment, felt bad that he wasn't more open about his feelings with her. *Oh, she knows how much I love her,* he said to himself, trying to minimize the guilt he felt, but then recognized what he was doing. It wasn't the first time he had tried to reason away his discomfort. One of the things that Frank's ex-wife would say to him was that she found him emotionally distant and often struggled to feel more connected with him. Frank had tried to convince himself that she was just "needy," but on some level he knew that there was truth to her words. It had always been hard for him to share from a deeper place inside, to step forward in his relationships in a fuller way. Yet it wasn't that he was without feelings. In fact, he felt things very deeply. But it was scary to open up and allow himself to be more vulnerable.

As Frank sat with his guilt, it pained him to think that the same distance might grow between him and Rachel—that over time she might end up feeling disconnected from him as well. He loved her so much and wanted her to know it, to be sure of it. He didn't want fear to hold him back or prevent this relationship from being all that it could be. Frank wanted to get it right this time.

That evening, as they often did, the two of them sat together and chatted. As Rachel told him about her day, Frank found himself just looking at her, watching her talk, noticing her mannerisms. He felt his heart swell with affection. She was so dear to him. He wanted to tell her how he felt, but then started to feel a little anxious. He could feel his heart beating faster and noticed that his hands were cold. Frank focused inward and tried to center himself. Then he went for it.

"You know, I was thinking about you today," he said.

"Really? What about?" Rachel asked.

"Um, I was just thinking about how . . . how wonderful you are. And, um . . . that I don't really tell you enough . . . how much I love you."

Rachel smiled wide. "Oh honey, that's so nice to hear." She moved closer to him, and they embraced.

As Frank was getting ready for bed, he thought about what he'd done. He was so pleased that he had pushed himself to open up a bit. It made him feel good. And he noticed that it wasn't so scary. *I need to do this more often,* he thought to himself.

✴

With mindful attention to his emotional experience, and a bit of determination, Frank is opening up to a deeper level of closeness in his relationship with Rachel. He's on his way to having more of the life he really wants.

IN OUR OWN WAY

As you can see from these different stories, when it comes to the process of opening up to and experiencing feelings, there are many different variations on a theme. At times, emotional experiences are fairly straightforward; at others, they're more complex. Sometimes feelings are readily apparent and easier to grasp; other times, we have to work harder to figure out what's going on inside. Now and then, the waters are difficult to maneuver; sometimes it's smooth sailing. We can expect that along the way there will inevitably be twists and turns, stops and starts, and roadblocks that will need to be dismantled and worked through. That's just the way it goes. But with a bit of effort and determination, we can find our way through.

As different as our experiences are, so too are the ways in which we may approach them. Each one of us is unique and at a different place on our emotional journey. Although the four steps are arranged in a sequence that you can use as a guide, you don't need to feel locked into them or that you have to follow the process all the way through each time. You may find that you move easily through one step and have a harder time with another or want to come back to the next step at another time. At other times, all the steps may not be necessary. It's up to you to discover your own way of doing things. A strategy that works well for one person might not work for someone else. That's why I've included a number of tools for you to choose from so that you can find what's best for you. There is no right or wrong. The important thing is that you stay in the game. That you keep coming back to your feelings, noticing where you are in the present moment, tuning in to what's going on inside you, and reaching out and trying to connect.

Remember, overcoming feelings phobia is a process. It takes practice and time. But the more you work on being aware of your feelings, taming your fear, seeing your feelings through, and sharing them with others, the easier it gets. Know that each time you find the courage to do things differently, to lean into your feelings instead of moving away from them, you're changing the way your brain works and loosening fear's grip on your emotional experience. You're expanding your capacity to feel and to be close to others. You're honoring your authentic self. You're transforming yourself and moving toward having the life you really want.

CHAPTER TAKE-HOME POINTS

- The four steps to overcoming feelings phobia and opening up have a directional flow to them and can be used as a guide.
- There is flexibility in the world of emotions.
- Opening up to our feelings may reveal unfinished business from the past that needs attention and care.
- If the going gets tough and you feel stuck, you might find it helpful to seek the assistance of a trained professional.
- Sometimes in our process, we don't recognize that our emotional response is defensive, but if we stay open and curious to our experience, we eventually get to our core feelings.
- Suppressed anger can affect our energy level and overall mood.
- When we encounter people's emotional limitations, it can help to practice empathic understanding of what it's like to be afraid of one's feelings.
- We may need to reconsider our hopes for a relationship and then decide how we'd like to proceed.
- Overcoming feelings phobia is a process that takes practice and time, but with a bit of effort and determination, you can find your way through.

CONCLUSION

Making a Choice

*Only those who will risk going too farCan possibly
find out how far one can go.*

—T. S. Eliot

IT WAS A BEAUTIFUL DAY IN JUNE. The afternoon sun streamed in
through the windows of my sister's living room, filling it with an
amber glow. I sat next to her on the couch, holding her new son,
my nephew Theo, only two weeks old. I looked down at this little
wonder sleeping in my arms and felt so moved. Not only blessed
to be present for this moment, but so grateful to be present in
my life.

As I gazed at this little boy, filled with such promise, I thought
about how much I had changed. Over the last three years, I'd
found the courage to face my fears and open up to a fuller
experience of my feelings. It wasn't easy at first, but the more
I was able to honor what was inside me and step into my life in
an authentic way, the stronger and more whole I felt. My worries and doubts receded, and in their place I experienced a new-
found sense of clarity and hope. I had stepped through a portal
into a new world alive with possibilities that had once seemed out
of reach. Now I was about to move halfway across the country,
leave my family and friends, and start a life in a different city with

someone I dearly loved. Pretty remarkable, given how much I'd once been held back by fear.

I looked over at my sister, and my heart began to ache. Soon I would have to say good-bye. I wondered how she was feeling about my leaving. I was about to ask, but then hesitated. *Maybe now's not the time,* I reasoned, *what with the new baby and all.* But I knew better. If I let this moment slip by, I'd miss an opportunity to connect more deeply. I didn't want that. I didn't want there to be anything left unspoken between us. I took a breath to calm myself and said, "So . . . um . . . I'm wondering how you're feeling about me leaving?"

"Not good," she answered, smiling slightly, and looked away. Silence for a moment. Then she looked back at me, her eyes filling with tears, and said, "I mean . . . I'm really going to miss you."

"I know . . . I know . . . ," I said, as I reached out to put my hand on hers, tears streaming down my cheeks. "It's so hard to leave. I'm going to miss you so much." We cried together.

I felt so close to my sister in that moment, sitting next to her, our hearts wide open. Saddened, but also so full of love and gratitude. Not one feeling, but several. And space enough for all of it. My life, richly felt. Meaningful in a new and profound way.

❋

Life is full of choices. You can choose to listen to your feelings or avoid them. You can choose whether to be present with what's inside you or numb yourself out. You can choose whether to open up, speak what's in your heart, move closer and connect with the people in your life, or let fear hold you back.

Every moment is full of the promise of something greater. Greater awareness. Greater vitality. Greater closeness. It's all within your reach.

This book gives you the tools to get there. Let these steps guide you, and know that I'm rooting for you. Hear my voice encouraging you onward.

When you feel that you're losing your way or that your fears are keeping you from getting the life you really want, just come back to your feelings, make room for them, listen to what's going on inside, and let them be your guide.

Living like you mean it is a choice—to step into the present moment with arms and heart wide open to a life fully felt, the life you really want.

If you've enjoyed what you just read and would like to learn more about getting the life you really want, you'll find several free resources to help you at http://www.LivingLikeYouMeanIt. com/resources.

APPENDIX: SEEKING PROFESSIONAL HELP

AT SOME POINT, YOU MAY BE INTERESTED in working with a trained professional to facilitate your progress. A therapist or coach can help you increase your awareness and experience of your feelings and overcome barriers that may be preventing you from being more emotionally present in your life. A therapist, in particular, can help you change more entrenched emotional patterns and work through unresolved issues from the past.

When you seek assistance, it's important to find someone who is skilled at and comfortable with helping people broaden and enhance their emotional experience. Do some research; get referrals from trusted others who have had a positive experience in therapy or coaching; interview professionals over the phone, ask them about their approach, what kind of training they've completed, and how long they've been practicing. When you find someone who seems like a good fit, have an initial consultation and see how it feels to you. It's essential that you work with some-one with whom you feel understood, connected, and safe, and confident in his or her ability to help you. You should be able to get a good sense of whether he or she is the right person to help you and if you're making progress fairly readily.

THERAPY

Although there are a number of different therapeutic approaches that emphasize emotional experience as a means to healing and change, I've chosen to include here only those with which I'm most familiar. You can learn more about them on their respective Web sites, where you will also find a directory of therapists. In addition, you can find therapists through the directories of national and local professional associations. Many states and provinces have more localized therapist directories, which might be helpful to you in your search.

Accelerated Experiential Dynamic Psychotherapy (AEDP) is a transformation-based model of psychotherapy that fosters new and healing emotional and relational experiences. Learn more about AEDP at http://www.aedpinstitute.com.

Emotion(ally) Focused Therapy (EFT) for individuals, couples, and families comprises short-term models of therapy that help people reorganize and expand their emotional experiences. See http://www.eft.ca and http://www.emotionfo cusedtherapy.org.

Experiential Dynamic Therapy (EDT) is an umbrella term for several different approaches that all help people overcome barriers to experiencing true feelings about the present and past. Go to http://www.iedta.net for further information.

Eye Movement Desensitization and Reprocessing (EMDR) is an information-processing model of psychotherapy that helps resolve symptoms of unresolved, disturbing life experiences. Learn more about EMDR at http://www.emdria.org.

COACHING

Life coaching can help you overcome obstacles to growth, maximize your potential, and get the life you really want. Life coaches have different areas of expertise (for example, creating more joy in your life, working through grief, increasing relationship fulfillment), so it's important to find someone who specializes in the areas that you're interested in further developing. You can learn more about coaching and get assistance finding a coach at the Web site for the International Coach Federation, http://www. coachfederation.org. In addition, the Center for Courageous Living offers coaching specific to the principles taught in this book. Visit us at http://www.cfcliving.com to learn more.

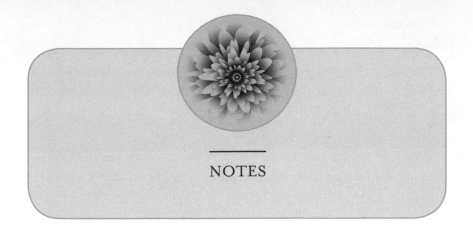

NOTES

Introduction
1. Goleman, D. (2006). *Social intelligence: The new science of human relationships.* New York: Bantam Dell.
2. Bowlby, J. (1988). *A secure base.* New York: Basic Books.

Chapter 1: To Feel or Not to Feel
1. McCullough, L. (1997). *Changing character.* New York: Basic Books.
2. LeDoux, J. (1996). *The emotional brain: The mysterious underpinnings of emotional life.* New York: Simon & Schuster.
3. Ibid.

Chapter 2: How the Heck Did I Get This Way?
1. LeDoux, J. (1996). *The emotional brain: The mysterious underpinnings of emotional life.* New York: Simon & Schuster.
2. Fosha, D. (2000). *The transforming power of affect.* New York: Basic Books.
3. Siegel, D. (2001). *The developing mind: How relationships and the brain interact to shape who we are.* New York: Guilford Press.
4. Ibid.
5. Schore, A. N. (1999). *Affect regulation and the origin of the self: The neurobiology of emotional development.* Mahwah, NJ: Erlbaum.
6. Lewis, M. (2000). The emergence of human emotions. In M. Lewis & J. M. Haviland-Jones (Eds.), *Handbook of emotions* (2nd ed., pp. 265–280). New York: Guilford Press.
7. Bowlby, J. (1988). *A secure base.* New York: Basic Books.
8. See Begley, S. (2007). *Train your mind, change your brain: How a new science reveals our extraordinary potential to transform ourselves.* New York: Ballantine Books; Davidson, R. J. (2000). Affective style,

psychopathology and resilience: Brain mechanisms and plasticity. *American Psychologist, 55,* 1193–1214; Doidge, N. (2007). *The brain that changes itself: Stories of personal triumph from the frontiers of brain science.* New York: Penguin Books.

9.   Goleman, D. (2006). *Social intelligence: The new science of human relationships.* New York: Bantam Dell.

10. Frost, R. (2002). *The poetry of Robert Frost.* New York: Henry Holt.

Chapter 3: Step One: Becoming Aware of Your Feelings

1.   Williams, M. G., Teasdale, J. D., Zindel, S. V., & Kabat-Zinn, J. (2007). *The mindful way through depression: Freeing yourself from chronic unhappiness.* New York: Guilford Press.

2.   Kabat-Zinn, J. (1994). *Wherever you go, there you are: Mindfulness meditation in everyday life.* New York: Hyperion.

3.   Safran, J. D., & Greenberg, L. S. (1991). *Emotion, psychotherapy, and change.* New York: Guilford Press.

Chapter 4: Step One: Continued: Becoming Aware of Your Defenses

1.   Briggs, D. C. (1977). *Celebrate your self.* New York: Doubleday.

2.   Gunaratana, B. H. (2002). *Mindfulness in plain English.* Boston: Wisdom Publications.

3.   Ezriel, H. (1952). Notes on psychoanalytic group therapy: II. Interpretation. *Research Psychiatry, 15,* 119.

Chapter 5: Step Two: Taming the Fear

1.   LeDoux, J. (1996). *The emotional brain: The mysterious underpinnings of emotional life.* New York: Simon & Schuster.

2.   Carnegie, D. Retrieved February 2008 from the Cyber Nation Web site: http://www.cybernation.com/victory/quotations/authors/quotes_carnegie_dale.html

3.   Lieberman, M. D., Eisenberger, N. I., Crockett, M. J., Tom, S. M., Pfeifer, J. H., & Way, B. M. (2007). Putting feelings into words: Affect labeling disrupts amygdala activity in response to affective stimuli. *Psychological Science, 18,* 421–428.

4.   Austin, J. H. (1999). *Zen and the brain: Toward an understanding of meditation and consciousness.* Cambridge, MA: MIT Press.

5.   Emmons, H. (2005). *The chemistry of joy: A three-step program for overcoming depression through Western science and Eastern wisdom.* New York: Simon & Schuster.

6.   Uvnas-Moberg, K. (1998). Oxytocin may mediate the benefits of positive social interaction and emotions. *Psychoneuroendocrinology, 23,* 819–835.

7. Kirsch, P., Esslinger, C., Chen, Q., Mier, D., Lis, S., Siddhanti, S., Gruppe, H., Mattay, V. S., Gallhofer, B., & Meyer-Lindenberg, A. (2005). Oxytocin modulates neural circuitry for social cognition and fear in humans. *Journal of Neuroscience, 25,* 11489–11493.

8. Frederickson, B. L., & Losada, M. F. (2005). Positive affect and the complex dynamics of human flourishing. *American Psychologist, 60,* 678–686.

9. Frederickson, B. L. (2005). Positive emotions. In C. R. Snyder & S. J. Lopez (Eds.), *Handbook of positive psychology* (pp. 120–134). New York: Oxford University Press.

10. Porges, S. (2006, March). *Love or trauma? How neural mechanisms mediate bodily responses to proximity and touch.* Paper presented at the Embodied Mind conference of the Lifespan Learning Institute, Los Angeles.

Chapter 6: Step Three: Feeling It Through

1. Fosha, D. (2000). *The transforming power of affect.* New York: Basic Books.

2. Greenberg, L. (2002). *Emotion-focused therapy: Coaching clients to work through their feelings.* Washington, DC: American Psychological Association.

3. McCullough, L. (1997). *Changing character.* New York: Basic Books.

4. Tavris, C. (1989). *Anger: The misunderstood emotion.* New York: Simon & Schuster.

5. Hanh, T. N. (2004). *Taming the tiger within: Meditations on transforming difficult emotions.* New York: Riverhead Books.

6. Rosenthal, N. E. (2002). *The emotional revolution: Harnessing the power of your emotions for a more positive life.* New York: Citadel Press.

7. Gendlin, E. T. (1981). *Focusing.* New York: Bantam Books.

8. Watkins, J. G., & Watkins, H. H. (1997). *Ego states: Theory and therapy.* New York: Norton.

9. Cozolino, L. (2002). *The neuroscience of psychotherapy: Building and rebuilding the human brain.* New York: Norton.

Chapter 7: Step Four: Opening Up

1. Bowlby, J. (1980). *Attachment and loss: Vol. 3. Loss, sadness, and depression.* New York: Basic Books.

2. Goleman, D. (1995). *Emotional intelligence: Why it can matter more than IQ.* New York: Bantam Books.

3. Beattie, M. (2002). *Choices: Taking control of your life and making it matter.* New York: HarperCollins.

4. Johnson, S. (2008). *Hold me tight: Seven conversations for a lifetime of love.* New York: Little, Brown.

5. Rizzolatti, G., & Sinigaglia, C. (2008). *Mirrors in the brain: How our minds share actions, emotions, and experience.* New York: Oxford University Press.

6. Jeffers, S. (1987). *Feel the fear and do it anyway.* New York: Ballantine Books.

Chapter 8: Putting It All Together

1. Freud, S. (1958). Mourning and melancholia. In J. Strachey (Ed. and Trans.), *The standard edition of the complete psychological works of Sigmund Freud* (Vol. 14, pp. 243–258). London: Hogarth Press. (Original work published 1915)

THE AUTHOR

Ronald J. Frederick, PhD, is a licensed psychologist and life coach with over fifteen years of experience helping people get the life they really want. A longtime proponent of the transforming power of emotion, he cofounded the Center for Courageous Living, which offers innovative therapy, coaching, and consulting. Noted for his warmth, humor, and engaging presentation style, he lectures and facilitates workshops nationally. An invited contributor to several professional books, he has also been quoted on CNN.com. In addition, Dr. Ron is a senior faculty member of the Accelerated Experiential Dynamic Psychotherapy (AEDP) Institute as well as the clinical supervisor of Park House, an outpatient program of Abbott Northwestern Hospital in Minneapolis. For more information about Dr. Ron and the Center for Courageous Living, go to http://www.cfcliving.com.

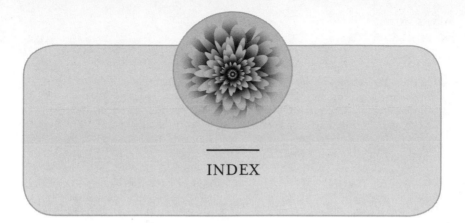

INDEX